RAISED
TO STAY

NATALIE RUNION

Persevering in Ministry When You Have
a Million Reasons to Walk Away

DAVID C COOK®

transforming lives together

RAISED TO STAY
Published by David C Cook
4050 Lee Vance Drive
Colorado Springs, CO 80918 U.S.A.

Integrity Music Limited, a Division of David C Cook
Brighton, East Sussex BN1 2RE, England

The graphic circle C logo is a registered trademark of David C Cook.

The website addresses recommended throughout this book are offered as a
resource to you. These websites are not intended in any way to be or imply an
endorsement on the part of David C Cook, nor do we vouch for their content.

Details in some stories have been changed to protect
the identities of the persons involved.

Bible credits are listed at the end of the book.

Library of Congress Control Number 2022951948
ISBN 978-0-8307-8460-8
eISBN 978-0-8307-8461-5

© 2023 Natalie Ryan Runion
Published in association with the literary agency of WordServe Literary
Group, Ltd., 7500 E Arapahoe Rd. Ste. 285, Centennial, CO 80112.

The Team: Susan McPherson, Stephanie Bennett,
James Hershberger, Jack Campbell, Susan Murdock
Cover Design: Joe Cavazos
Cover Author Bio Photo: Ashlee Kay Photography

Printed in the United States of America
First Edition 2023

1 2 3 4 5 6 7 8 9 10

031423

To my parents, my very first pastors
who taught me to love Jesus,
his Church, and his people

CONTENTS

FOREWORD

Though I'm often asked to write forewords for books, my schedule or the subject matter usually makes this honor impossible for me. But when Natalie asked me to add my voice to her book, I realized I couldn't say no. This one felt wildly different. She wasn't building a platform; she was calling forth the beauty of the Bride. I sensed this book could lead to a movement of healing and reformation.

Like many of you, I first noticed Natalie's offerings on the black-and-white boxes of the Raised to Stay memes. Each post is a tender blend of the prophetic and the practical. And I love that they are completely void of ego. I believe the things Natalie speaks resonate so deeply with so many because she has lived out every word. For it is one thing to have a message and quite another to be one.

I've had the privilege of living in the same city as Natalie and worshipping with her. She knows what she speaks of, because as you will discover, Natalie has seen the Church at its worst and yet believes that Jesus is up to the impossible task of loving his bride into her best.

> Christ's love makes the church whole. His words
> evoke her beauty. Everything he does and says
> is designed to bring the best out of her, dressing
> her in dazzling white silk, radiant with holiness.
> (Eph. 5:26–27 MSG)

We are a long way from the reality of this scripture.

It doesn't take a prophet to realize the Church at large is broken rather than whole. For many, her stained-glass beauty shattered into broken shards that embedded themselves into the souls of those who walked through her doors. These are the very ones who are now afraid to step within her doors again. There is no hiding the fact that her once-white garments have been soiled by decades of pride, injustice, and perversion. The once radiance of a holy bride has been stripped down to an ugly parody of legalism.

It is daunting to believe that we could ever dare to be part of changing this imagery. Are we willing to follow in the footsteps of our wounded healer? To do so will require a potent mix of faith, hope, and love. It will take no small amount of courage to prophesy what the Church could be rather than criticize what she has become. It will be easier to flip the table rather than set one for others. Conversely, at times it will be easier to stay in something that is unhealthy than to leave in faith, believing that God has anointed us to rise and build something healthy in another place.

There are so many things that need to be deconstructed, but if this deconstruction is done without a heart for reconstruction, then it is merely destruction. The good news is that we are not

alone in this hard and holy conversation. The words of the prophet
Isaiah support this:

> Come now, let us reason together, says the LORD:
> though your sins are like scarlet,
>> they shall be as white as snow;
> though they are red like crimson,
>> they shall become like wool. (Isa. 1:18 ESV)

This book is an invitation for each of us to heal so that we
can return to a place of reason. Whether you choose to leave or to
stay, you are loved either way. Life has taught me that we are all
prodigals in one manner or another. The important thing to know
is that you are watched for, celebrated, and always welcomed home
by our heavenly Father.

Lisa Bevere

New York Times bestselling author and minister

Messenger International cofounder

INTRODUCTION

I have known the Church and her people my entire life. I suppose that's why you, reader, feel familiar to me though we are most likely perfect strangers. I wrote this with you in mind, my brothers and sisters in the faith who have journeyed far and wide in our wandering and wondering and still find ourselves here in the wrestling with Jesus and the Church.

Growing up amid all the church services, revivals, camp meetings, weekly potlucks, weddings, funerals, and holiday events, I saw my church family more often than blood relatives. Through junior high and high school, my family lived in the church parsonage, a house for the pastor and his family that sat on the church property. I loved seeing members of the congregation come and go throughout the week and retrieving the little treats the older women would leave for us on the porch or the cards in the screen door.

When I look over my journals from that time of my life, it was clear I loved the Church. I wanted to be a youth pastor, and I led worship anytime I was given the opportunity. I wrote songs, practiced sermons in my bedroom mirror with a curling iron as a microphone, and spent hours writing heartfelt prayers asking the Lord to show me his plan for my life. We were the first to arrive at the church building and the last to leave, but I never minded. It was home.

As the pastor's daughter, I was the model youth group kid who sang in the choir, taught Sunday school classes, went on mission trips, led worship around the campfire, and listened only to Christian music, since most of our secular CDs were literally burned in the annual "secular music is from Satan" Wednesday-night-service object lesson. I wore a promise ring my dad got me when I turned fourteen, read *I Kissed Dating Goodbye*, and wore one-piece bathing suits at every pool party. There were days it felt like I would snap under the weight of all the expectations and rules, and I found myself behaving just so I wouldn't disappoint anyone. I plunged into a cycle of people pleasing, seeking approval from leaders and peers and setting unrealistic expectations on myself and others.

As I grew up and developed my own sense of discernment, I began to catch glimpses behind the giant curtain of ministry. Slowly I realized that the place I loved wasn't as perfect as I'd always thought. And I was devastated when my own family fell victim to the dreaded "church hurt," a disease I'd heard about but never experienced firsthand.

The summer before my senior year in high school, my parents, younger sister, and I were called into an early Sunday morning meeting where, much to our surprise, it was announced that we would leave the church immediately without any explanation or choice in the matter. I'll never forget standing in front of the congregation that very same Sunday, my father speechless as we were forced to say goodbye, unable to defend ourselves or help them come to a better understanding of what was happening.

We said goodbye to our church family, the people who had raised me, prayed over me, threw birthday parties for us, and shared in every celebration and loss. That same week we packed up the parsonage and drove miles out of town to a horse farm owned by a family friend. We spent much of my senior year of high school living in a one-bedroom efficiency apartment over a barn.

The Church Who Built Me

I remember tossing and turning on a mattress on the floor next to my parents' bed that I shared with my younger sister, the soundtrack to *My Best Friend's Wedding* playing through flimsy 1997 foam headphones. I could hear the horses stomping below me in their stalls, and I wanted to join them in my own temper tantrum. It was from this space that I watched my dad search for jobs for the first time in my life, the sound of squeaking yellow highlighter circling the want ads waking me up in the morning.

It was the first time I'd ever felt true anger at the Church, the first time I'd ever felt betrayed and utterly forgotten. I had never questioned God or the Church like this before and it was terrifying to feel like I was divorcing the Church who had built me. I didn't know who I was if I wasn't a pastor's kid, and I didn't know how to go to church like normal people went to church. I felt orphaned by an institution that was supposed to love and shelter me.

Earlier that year I had been accepted to a Christian college, but that summer, I made a very quick decision to attend a major state university instead. When I left home that fall, I was still heartbroken over the church hurt our family had endured. I moved into a coed dorm with a Jewish roommate who loved Indigo Girls and carbohydrates. I started to find out who I was in this new season of life.

College Freshman Natalie liked writing and working out. She liked dance music and poetry and '80s-themed parties. She was obsessed with bold fashion choices and makeup. She was eccentric and a little irrational, unconventional, and artistic yet entrepreneurial. I became a science major with atheist professors who would pick me out of a crowd of three hundred and make me debate everything from Creationism to the Big Bang Theory until I was left in a heap of my own humiliation. It was there that I would spend the next five years trying to convince myself I didn't want anything to do with ministry or the Church.

So yeah, I've wanted to quit. Trust me, I've tried to quit on multiple occasions, and if I'm really honest, I want to quit a little bit every single day. If you're reading this because you or someone you care about is wanting to quit too, you're in good company. Even now as a pastor myself, I have days I question God and wrestle with my relationships with him and his Church. I still have moments I'm ready to throw in the towel—and you know what? That doesn't make me a bad person or a sinner. It makes me human, and if you've been there, it makes you human too.

It is possible to question behaviors and beliefs we have seen in the church, religious organizations, and in Christians without quitting Jesus or divorcing the family of God. Jesus is right there in our wandering, wondering, and wrestling.

Saints and Skeptics

Listen closely. Can you hear it? That cross is so loud. The empty grave is even louder. The cross speaks of a God who keeps his promises, and the grave screams of a Christ who finishes what he starts. And in all my questions, mostly private wrestling, I have never been able to get away from what I said yes to when I was seven years old. I didn't say yes to emotional hype, programs, lights, worship concerts, big stadiums, large corporations, ladder climbing, and ditch digging.

I said yes to Jesus in the simplest way, at the foot of my little white poster bed on a Sunday night after a children's church service, the cold hardwood floor beneath my knees and my mom by my side. I said yes and I never looked back. Because I didn't say yes to religion or church politics or an organization. I said yes to a Jesus who made me and loved me and who is proud of me. I said yes to a hope of what that empty tomb stands for even on the days I doubt the most.

Even on the days when I'm feeling like Doubting Thomas and I get a little sarcastic and say, "Fine, show me your nail-scarred hands."

Even on the days I deny him three times, I'm not fooling anyone. My life, my songs, my calling, they betray me because it's clear to everyone around me that I have spent many hours walking closely with Jesus—and I'm not ready to leave him or his church behind, no matter how angry or hurt I am.

> If you're reading this because you or someone you care about is wanting to quit too, you're in good company.

I have no doubt that if we were to sit around my kitchen table with a cup of coffee telling our stories, we would have exhaustive lists of why we're ready to throw in the towel and call it quits. There would be a lot of "uh-huh" and nodding of heads, there would most likely be tears and possibly a few bad words that we'd apologize about later (or not). We'd probably laugh a little at some of the common items on our lists and then sit in silence with each other because, dang, it's hard to see each other hurt.

For some of you, every political year leaves you more disenchanted with the local church. For others, it's the inability to have hard and holy conversations from the pulpit on race, the LGBTQ community, divorce, pornography, and gender equality. For many, the Covid-19 pandemic gave you a reason to stay home on Sunday mornings and it's been alarmingly easy to disengage and find more comfort in the online platforms of those wrestling with similar questions and frustrations.

I see all of you. God sees you too.

I often think of Paul, one of Jesus' very own disciples, who saw miracle after miracle and even he, in his own journey, was begging God to make it all stop. We find Paul confessing what life was like following Jesus after the resurrection, and it certainly wasn't big stages, fancy hotels, book deals, and awards. It wasn't large crowds, fan letters, bright lights, and jets. Choosing Jesus and choosing to carry the Gospel, choosing to love people, it was hard.

In 2 Corinthians 11, Paul talks about being robbed, beaten, misunderstood, and betrayed by his own people. He then goes on to say he has been shipwrecked *three times*. At this point I have to ask the question. *Paul, why do you keep getting back in the boat?*

Why do any of us?

I have to believe Paul got back in because he knew the reward would be greater than the risk. If he quit, he'd never know what or who was waiting for him on the other side.

I have had recent seasons where I considered going back to my first job as a gym teacher because crazy children are easier than wrestling and fighting with adult evangelicals. I can remember kids getting into fights in my gymnasium over a favorite basketball or position in line, and that was normal. Children fight. Children never think there's enough to go around. Children act out. But when you see it happening in the church among Christian adults who are supposed to know better, it's disappointing. It is extremely alarming when adults start fighting, when leaders start hoarding leadership opportunities and climbing ladders because they are afraid there won't be enough. It's maddening when adults who know better behave like children and act out rather than have hard and holy conversations with one another that will bring unity and restoration.

Yet as I slowly step into my calling, I feel my frustration turn to holy lament as the Lord breaks my heart for his people and I learn to wrestle with them. With my own thoughts and questions. With him.

Like Paul, we find ourselves telling stories and making a list of all the horrible things that have happened to us while trying to do good things, and we're a little bit amazed we've survived it all. When I look back over my own story, I'm in awe that I'm still here holding on—even though I've begged God to let me go.

He has a stack of my resignation letters that he never accepted, oh but he read them. They are scribbled with complaints of bad work environment, toxic leadership, narcissistic oversights, inappropriate coworkers, and impossible work conditions. I have a million reasons to walk away from it all, but there is this one reason that I can't shake: Jesus.

Paul knew the only reason he was able to talk about all the things that were exposing his weakness was because in it showed the great strength of his God. Paul confesses in 2 Corinthians 12:8 that "three times I pleaded with the Lord to take it [a thorn in his flesh to keep him humble] away from me" (NIV).

What was God's response?

"My grace is sufficient for you, for my power is made perfect in weakness" (v. 9 NIV).

We learn through these scriptures that it's okay to admit we've been hurt, overlooked, rejected, and misled by people we placed our trust in. That doesn't make us weak or incapable, it doesn't disqualify us from leadership. We learn from Paul that with every question, every attempt to resign from this madness, every opportunity to quit, that in our weakness we see the power of God.

And I want Christ's power to rest on me. For when we are most weak, he is so strong (2 Cor. 12:10).

Literally, the only thing that can stop us from doing what God has called us to do is if we quit and let those questions become louder than the cross and our guilt louder than the grave.

And gosh, guilt and disappointment and inadequacy can be excruciatingly loud. I once had a counselor tell me that anger is a secondary emotion as I cried on her floor in a heap of hot, angry tears. Yes, I was mad. But mostly I was embarrassed and felt misunderstood and misrepresented. Knowing this, I was able to lie in my own weakness and let Jesus step in to speak his Word over me. To replace the lies with his truth and rewrite the script to my life with words of life and hope, not death and destruction.

Consider these questions with me:

- How would you describe your relationship with Jesus? How would you describe your relationship with the Church?
- What has been said or done to you in your life that has become louder than the voice of your Father?
- What lies have you believed?

Sometimes we just need to be reminded that we are deeply loved and to stop being so hard on ourselves. We can be our own worst critics! God is for us and he is with us. He is so strong in our weakness; he gives us perfect peace in our biggest storms. It's been over twenty-five years since my family moved to that farm, and it's only now that I write and say to you with confidence, "His grace is sufficient for you." Let that promise rest over you. His grace is sufficient for you.

Together, we will take this journey toward trusting him again, knowing that people will fail us, but the love of God never fails. This is what makes me take a second look when I'm ready to run, what gives me second thoughts about quitting ministry and the Church when I feel like I have a million reasons to walk away.

I am still learning to listen closely for the roar of the resurrection when I feel as if I'll be consumed by the grave of doubt and shame. I've been comforted in remembering my yes to Jesus as a child and the reminder that I can come to him now with that same innocence and he will hold on to me tightly in my temper tantrums, screaming fits, and silent treatments. In my weakest moments, red faced and my heart clanging in my chest, he is constant and true like a good father.

I'm not suggesting we stop asking questions or raising doubts. No, we have to *keep* asking questions. We have to *keep* wrestling with ourselves and wrestling with others. God is in it all. What we can't do is give up. We can't quit.

You're probably asking, why does it matter if I choose to walk away from ministry or if I choose to stop attending church or calling myself a Christian? What if I'm ready to walk away from Jesus altogether? Why does a perfect stranger care if I quit? We can't quit because if we quit …

We will never see God work it all out for our good.

We won't get to see that beauty from those ashes.

We won't get to experience the living hope we have in Jesus Christ.

We won't see what happens when we let him fight for us.

We may not witness reconciliation and redemption in our story and the lives of others.

We won't know the exhilarating exhaustion of running this race and hearing, "Well done, good and faithful servant."

In 1 Peter 1:3–7, we read:

What a God we have! And how fortunate we are to have him, this Father of our Master Jesus! Because Jesus was raised from the dead, we've been given a brand-new life and have everything to live for, including a future in heaven—and the future starts now! God is keeping careful watch over us and the future. The Day is coming when you'll have it all—life healed and whole.

I know how great this makes you feel, even though you have to put up with every kind of aggravation in the meantime. Pure gold put in the fire comes out of it *proved* pure; genuine faith put through this suffering comes out *proved* genuine. When Jesus wraps this all up, it's your faith, not your gold, that God will have on display as evidence of his victory. (MSG)

I love that part of the scripture that says one day we will be *healed and whole*. That is why we cannot quit: one day he will make all things right and new.

We keep our eyes fixed on Jesus, the author and perfecter of our faith, and we're honest with our fears as he calms the waters around us. He won't fail us!

> We can't quit because if we quit we will never see God work it all out for our good. We won't get to see that beauty from those ashes.

Oh, and about those letters of resignation we routinely send him? He holds on to them to remind us that he wastes nothing, that our questioning and pain and worries and frustrations don't disqualify us or become our identity. Rather, these experiences give us credentials to tell others it's going to be okay. When you've survived three shipwrecks, people pay attention to where you've been and where you're going.

And we'll finish this race together. We will get tired, we may get a cup of water, we might need to tie our shoelaces or take a restroom break, but we finish this race.

His grace is sufficient for each and every one of us.

Are you ready to start running again?

In it to finish it,

Natalie

PART I

THE HURT

CHAPTER 1

WONDERERS AND WANDERERS

"Not all those who wander are lost."[1]

J. R. R. Tolkien

I went to college in the fall of 1998, one year after my family's great exodus from the Church. I was making life-altering decisions in a strange new world of academics and coed dormitories when just a year prior my mom had been folding my laundry and my dad packing my school lunches with little notes inside.

Even as I explored this new world and formed new friendships, much of my mind was still rooted in what had happened to my family and what I'd left behind. Every night for months, I stayed up way past midnight working on a book, *the* book in my mind, about being a pastor's kid. I went into great detail, naming names, places, and specific scenarios that had played out not even a year previously, the wounds still fresh and bleeding. I wrote and rewrote the chapters so many times it was like opening an old scab with every edit.

I would sit at the little built-in wooden desk in the dorm room, my face glowing in the green light of my brand-new PC as the neon cursor blinked to the rhythm of my roommate's snores. In the darkness I traced the names of strangers etched into the desk's wood, the names of those who had called our dorm room, Emerson 159, home. I wondered where they were, what they were doing, and if our dorm room that often smelled like stale pizza and cheap beer (don't worry, you guys; I drank Diet Coke) had been part of changing their lives for the better. Did they figure out who they were, what they wanted to do, and who they wanted to become in that tiny space, or did it take much longer to get there?

For nearly six months I had been writing and laboring over every word, until one fall night in that college dorm room I did a final review and with great satisfaction typed:

THE END.

THE END of an era.

THE END of a call.

THE END of a lifetime of ministry.

THE END of eighteen years of people who said they cared walking away.

THE END of seeing my parents in pain.

THE END of being judged.

THE END of the Church rejecting us.

THE END of gossip.

THE END of unkept promises.

THE END of religion.

THE END OF NATALIE, PASTOR'S KID.

I jumped on my bike and pedaled like a crazy woman to the printing lab, where I was met with a few sleepy graduate students working late into the night. I pulled out my dining card with freshly loaded, hard-earned money, knowing that to print this book would take every penny on it. I put the disk (yes, guys, we still used floppy disks then!) into the computer, and for thirty minutes I impatiently watched each line roll out in very expensive ink: my very first book, *My Initials Are Not P.K.*

I sent the book to the only place I knew to send it, a large Christian ministry that produced books and magazines on all types of topics. In my naivete, youthful optimism, and pride, I was convinced they would receive the pages and call me immediately with a major book deal that would put me on a trajectory toward fame and speaking gigs.

I stalked the dormitory mail room for months, assuming the manuscript had gotten lost or misplaced because *surely* they wouldn't pass up this masterpiece. It wasn't until that spring of my freshman year in college, roughly six months later, that I got a response. It was a single-page letter attached to the manuscript simply saying, "No, thank you." I scanned farther down to see the person had written a bit more. This hadn't come from a secretary or auto-generated rejection robot.

At the bottom of the page were the handwritten words: "Your story isn't finished yet."

We All Wander

By the time I got to college, my struggle with the Church and my faith, like many of my Christian peers', was silent. Like someone out in the water who appears from a distance to be doing just fine but in reality is drowning. I wasn't crying out for help or rebelling to get attention, but every day I was wrestling with big questions that I didn't have the guts to ask anyone. For the first time in my life, I wasn't certain of exactly what I believed or why. I wasn't surrounded by lifelong Christians.

My roommate was Jewish and we would talk a little about our faith, but I was rusty in my Old Testament trivia, and any New Testament discussion that took my Jesus off the cross and out of the tomb seemed foreign to her, so we settled on conversations of our common love of cafeteria cereal and boot-legged jeans. There was little evidence of evangelical life in this strange new world, and what I witnessed did little to comfort me. I'd frequently pass men standing on the corners of major intersections spinning signs that said, "You're going to hell," who got into screaming arguments with students on the street as I watched in horror.

Every day I met people with different religious backgrounds and moral belief systems who aggressively challenged mine, and I was embarrassed when I couldn't defend why I didn't drink, sleep with my boyfriend, or cheat on exams. I met amazing people who didn't believe in God and yet were kind, loving, giving, and compassionate, including those from the LGBTQ community who I had been taught to fear and who, it turned out, were gentle and terrific listeners and made me laugh until I cried.

Some of my best friends were good Christian people from amazing families who could drink alcohol responsibly, cussed a little, and loved a good cigar, and I was jealous they had found a loophole in the religious system. I met Jehovah's Witnesses and young Mormon men on mission, and we'd all sit together at lunch, pretty sure the others were wrong, but having fun debating and telling stories regardless.

In my wandering I learned to let my heart break repeatedly and how to love people well.

Because of these new relationships and intentional conversations, I found myself questioning the rules and religious rituals I had adopted growing up simply by association. I felt more loved by perfect strangers than those in our church community back home who were still talking about us and whispering when we walked into a room.

I attended standing-room-only campus events with classmates where topics were debated as students sat in open windows and listened from the lawn. I would leave those gatherings asking really important questions. Why did I believe what I believe? What if I was wrong? What if all these other people who were living without so many rules were actually right? Is heaven real? Is God real? Is the Bible relevant for today's world? Did God really say that?

For the first time, I was wandering. It was messy, uncomfortable, clumsy, and emotional as I tried to detangle myself from religion and still hold on to the Jesus I knew.

As I was starting my senior year in college, not knowing what was coming or where I was going, I hit a wall. In one of my journal entries from that time, I wrote:

"I long to be surrounded in the warmth and safety of my teenage years where your biggest problem was what you were wearing to school the next day or if you'd pass that hot guy on the way to class. But it's not like that anymore, I'm cynical and weathered and for the first time **I want out.***"*

Have you ever been there? Feeling like you just want out? Like you want to scream at the top of your lungs, "Stop the train, I want to get off!"?

I continued, *"These shattered dreams, storms, they won't stop, and I've never wanted to quit like I want to quit right now. How did it get like this? I can't sleep right, I can't eat … Why am I always battling and watching things crumble? I'm not asking for a miracle; I'm just asking if you can hear me."*

In the pages of my journals I documented every secret question, processed my guilt for doubting and being afraid, and watched myself clumsily navigate through personal deserts and barren seasons. I wrote down the things I was too afraid to confess out loud.

I know you may not be living the story you wanted either. I know God might be silent right now. You may feel like you're wandering on your own in a world that has made some faulty promises with people who have let you down, but hold on with me for just a bit longer as we take this journey together in the chapters ahead. We're not in a hurry, and God is working in our wrestling even now.

Jesus Wandered Too

Sometimes, even when others can't see it, our wandering is the very thing that is meant to lead us home to God. I think of the story in Luke 2:41–52, where Jesus, just a boy, knew he had a call on his life, a mandate, a specific assignment that only he could fulfill, and he found himself on a journey with his parents to Jerusalem for the Feast of Passover. At twelve years old he didn't need a career day to figure out where his life was headed; he was drawn to the temple and the teachers and he wandered from his parents to sit and learn from those doing the very thing he knew he was called to do.

The whole time Jesus was in the temple, of course, his parents were searching all over for him, assuming he was somewhere among the pilgrims, relatives, or friends. They were furious that he'd run off and they were frantic to find him. People panic when others wander. And yet the passage notes that "the teachers were all quite taken with [Jesus], impressed with the sharpness of his answers" (v. 47 MSG). Those on the outside were looking for a lost Jesus, but those to whom he had wandered welcomed him in. What a validating moment it must have been for Jesus to finally feel like he was sitting among those who understood him! Even these scholars could see that at twelve years old, Jesus had something special and unique.

I think many of us wander off to find our people, who we are, what we believe, and if anyone believes in us. We're not looking to go rogue; we're looking to be heard, validated, and understood.

Lost and Found

I don't think any of us start this process of wondering and wandering hoping to get lost. While I'm not suggesting we spend our entire lives in this place, I am suggesting we give ourselves and others grace and time to find the answers we're looking for, and that we trust God knows exactly where we are.

Not too long ago our youngest daughter got lost at the mall. It was the most terrified I've ever been as a parent, and within seconds our panic was at an all-time high. Other moms heard us screaming her name and an army of women dispersed throughout the building, searching for my child. Security guards were asking what she was wearing, and fear was washing over me as seconds turned into minutes.

I'll never forget the image of my husband bursting through the glass doors with her in his arms and the sound of relief that came from all the women when we found her. She had gotten separated from my husband, walked through the wrong doors, and couldn't find her way back to us.

The whole time we were looking for her, I kept hearing the Lord say, "I can see her, it's okay." She had simply walked through the wrong doors.

We are all at different points in our wandering with Jesus. We each have different experiences, unique passions and personalities that impact our journey, and nobody can do this hard and holy work for us. We walk through wrong doors, sometimes by accident and other times by choice, and every single time he meets us on the other side.

> Many of us wander off to find our people, who we are, what we believe, and if anyone believes in us. We're not looking to go rogue; we're looking to be heard, validated, and understood.

Even when we feel the furthest from his hand, his eyes never leave our path. His grace is always with us. And the Lord, his gaze always on us, dispatches his angel army with the passion of ten thousand moms looking for one of their own, and they don't stop until we're back in his arms.

He will leave the ninety-nine to find the one.

It's okay if sometimes we're the one. We all wander off from time to time, and God does not give up on us if we're gone a day or fifty years.

He doesn't shame us or scold us. He celebrates our return because what was lost has been found.

He still calls us son and daughter.

Even Jesus had a mom. I imagine Mary felt a combination of anger and relief upon finding Jesus after a day of looking for him. It's every mom's nightmare to lose your child, but I mean, come on, you can't lose the Son of God. I love *The Message* version of this passage when Mary reprimanded Jesus: "Young man, why have you done this to us? Your father and I have been half out of our minds looking for you" (Luke 2:48). Yes, Jesus had a very specific assignment, but he was still young and still needed his mom. She wasn't holding him back; she was taking him home until he was fully released to lead the disciples, perform miracles, and ultimately save the people of God.

I imagine Jesus sheepishly walking away from those men he admired, kicking little dirt piles as he left the temple and headed home with the occasional "Mommmmmmm," as she cleaned him up along the way.

This story ends with Jesus going back to Nazareth with his mom and dad where he "lived obediently with them. His mother held these things dearly, deep within herself. And Jesus matured, growing up in both body and spirit, blessed by both God and people" (Luke 2:51–52 MSG).

It wouldn't be until the wedding feast where Jesus turned the water into wine that his mom fully released him into his God-given assignment. He was no longer a child aimlessly wandering for answers and purpose but a man who was about to step into his authority that no human or scheme of hell could stop.

The good news for you and me is that even in our wandering God has never changed his mind about us. He is so very sure of who we are in him and who he has created us to be, even on the days we feel lost, unheard, or like we're being held back.

The Story Isn't Over

The beauty of wandering is that we find all sorts of things we didn't expect to find along the way, and the journey becomes a part of our unique story. My own personal wandering would lead me from the classroom back into the sanctuary, where I met some incredible people—some who knew Jesus, some who were getting to know him, and others who were walking away. Part of my journey was finding that I really did love God and the Church, even though I carried scars and wounds that were still actively healing.

After graduating college, I went on a wild goose chase trying to find my own ministry outside of being a pastor's kid. Leading worship was my entrance into many opportunities. I wasn't handed a ministry of two thousand people; instead, I would sit behind pianos in nursing homes and small group meetings, women's events and small church camps, and lead worship like I had around all those youth group bonfires years before.

I learned to listen to people, really listen to where they were and to help them detangle and unravel from some of the very lies I had believed that had led to my own wandering and wondering. When we as the Church embark on our own faith journey and admit to having our own big questions and doubts, it's amazing how much grace and patience we carry for those in the middle of their own.

After college, I spent most of my twenties teaching physical education while also working part time for different churches and organizations. When I was thirty-three, I was given the opportunity to enter into full-time ministry, where I served five years at a large church in Cincinnati leading worship for a congregation of what they called "the most of these." They were the top business professionals in our city, millionaires who loved networking, loved God, and wanted their friends who had been taken advantage of by religious institutions to meet a Jesus who loved them for who they were, not how much money they had.

For this population, their greatest journey would be from their head to their heart, that eighteen-inch drop from knowing about Jesus to truly knowing him. It was the most challenging role I had ever accepted because most of these men and women were skeptics and critics sitting in pews that I had only known to be filled with compliant saints.

Every week I was given ten minutes to lead worship, knowing that most of them were watching me through a lens of "prove to me this Jesus is real." One man in particular, a well-known bank owner who loved cigars and a good whiskey, would stand in the foyer until the music was over. As I was placing my mic back on the stand, I would see his looming shadow enter slyly through the sanctuary doors and take his seat in the back row.

One Sunday, as I was leading "Revelation Song," I felt a nudge like I was supposed to keep singing the chorus, but when I looked up at the clock, I saw we were out of time. Rather than singing the chorus again, I quickly ended the song to make sure I didn't go over my allowed time slot. As I was leaving the church that morning, the banker was waiting for me at the front doors, a scowl on his face, arms crossed.

I said hello and tried to pass by quickly, but he stopped me, gently catching my arm with his giant hands. He pulled his sunglasses down and I saw his eyes and nose were red with emotion.

He said, "You rushed me today." I was confused. I had rushed him? When? Doing what?

He continued, "You know, during that one song that said 'holy' a lot. I wasn't done singing and you stopped the song."

And then I remembered that moment on the stage when I felt like I was supposed to repeat the chorus and I didn't because I was afraid.

He had been standing in the back of the room during worship that day, rather than his usual spot in the foyer.

On this particular Sunday in his wandering, he found himself in the back of the sanctuary.

I immediately felt my heart sink and my eyes fill with tears as our separate journeys with Jesus collided, the pastor's kid who sometimes just wanted to get out of a worship set without any mistakes and the banker who was just starting to meet Jesus.

I hugged him, my arms barely able to get over his huge shoulders, and I apologized for not recognizing the space he needed in that moment. He wouldn't have understood my Christian language for what he was feeling at that time, but I knew an apology would be a good start.

A few months later I resigned to take a worship position out of state, and on my last Sunday, this man sat in the first pew, front and center. Each week he had started journeying a little closer and a little closer to the platform.

And on that Sunday, my last Sunday in that beautiful sanctuary surrounded by critics who had become my friends, I led "Revelation Song" one last time. The music was swelling, and I stood in awe at their worship, some quiet and reserved, others clapping and whistling as the song came to a close. I felt it once more, *sing it again*, and this time I listened. I cued the band and the music built up one more time, and the banker stood on that front pew giving me a thumbs-up like a proud dad watching his daughter.

You never know who you'll meet when you don't quit.

You'll never know who won't quit on you.

You never know who needs you along their journey and that you probably need them too.

The book I started at eighteen years old, that scathing exposé of kicking butts and naming names, was never meant to be published. Whoever wrote the rejection letter was right. My story wasn't over. But it was the beginning of giving myself permission to be angry, get mad, and wrestle in a way I had never wrestled with God and the Church.

I don't know where you are in your wandering, but I want you to know that you are deeply loved and seen by God. There are a lot of voices speaking over you as you scroll social media looking for those who will listen to you and validate your season or assignment. Many voices will point fingers at people who hurt you and encourage you to do the same, but I challenge you to look for those who will sit with you and remind you who you are in Christ.

> You never know who you'll
> meet when you don't quit.

Who are those people you admire? Who walks with Jesus in a way that doesn't make you feel judged but embraces your part of the journey and wants to join you on the adventure? Who shows you a Jesus who is patient and kind, slow to anger and quick in love? These are the people we look for along the way.

As we take this journey together, I hope you find that in me. A safe place to wander, wonder, and wrestle with someone who still very much does the same.

Don't stop dreaming. Don't stop wandering.

We've got places to go.

What to Expect

In our time together I promise to be transparent with you regarding my personal wandering, wondering, and wrestling with the Church. I'll take you on my own journey of fighting for a Church

I believe exists as we look at a few of our favorite Bible characters and stories and watch how God used wandering, wondering, and wrestling to bring his people through shipwrecks, pits, and storms to reveal his power in their lives. We will also examine the relationships between the disciples and those they brought alongside them in ministry and how even our very own Judas can bring us closer to Jesus. We will meet others just like you and me who have struggled in their relationships with the Church and still love Jesus as they navigate hard and holy spaces every single day.

It might be helpful to keep a notebook or journal close by; take your time processing what God is speaking to you. Write notes in the margins, underline, highlight, take a screenshot of something that sticks out to you. We're all on this journey together, and God wants us to truly know him as we uncover hard and holy spaces between these pages.

CHAPTER 2

STAINED-GLASS
WINDOWS

*"The easiest thing to do is throw a rock. It's a
lot harder to create a stained-glass window.
I used to get upset at the people who threw
rocks but now I'd rather spend my time
building the stained-glass windows."*[2]

Jon Foreman

I have always been a wanderer at heart, anxious to explore a world
outside of my pastor's kid bubble, and even now I am often restless
for what might be next. I am curious about culture, desperate for
adventure, and as a pastor's kid I wanted to believe there was life
beyond pews and pulpits. I wanted to know if my life, my identity,
my initials were more than just Natalie, P.K.

It was on my first mission trip at eighteen years old that I fell
in love with traveling and meeting new people from all around
the world. My dad used to tell me if I ever found myself alone
and afraid in a new city to look for a church. I found this advice

odd knowing how much pain the church had caused him and our family over the years; what I know now is he was teaching me to look up and not inside one particular church building or denomination. He was teaching me to look for Jesus and ways to be Jesus to everyone I met.

In the darkest cities, most abandoned towns, or while walking crowded streets in a bustling metropolis, I always found a church steeple towering into the night, a warm beacon shining bright like the familiar porchlight of a childhood home.

In my early twenties, I chased my love for acting, musical theater, and big cities to New York City. There I found old cathedrals, the wooden pews digging into my lower back as I listened to the heater crackling and wind howling eerily through pipe organs looming at the helm, the distinguished gatekeeper of holy ground.

Then there was the tiny one-room schoolhouse in North Carolina I discovered while on location shooting a TV series, just one of my many wanderings to finding a Jesus I was desperate to meet. Hidden off an old country path, it was furnished with a bell that rang every hour to the tune of "'Tis So Sweet to Trust in Jesus" and an out-of-tune upright piano with tattered red back hymnals scattered throughout the historic pews.

My love for the beach led me to a Hispanic congregation in Florida who taught me how to sing in Spanish, and I followed the mountains to a Messianic church in Denver that had me dancing in a circle hand in hand, laughing and shouting until I almost passed out from altitude sickness. I can remember the Pentecostal church in Kentucky where I led the singing of the same song for three hours followed by a southern potluck dinner of homemade buttery goodness.

Finally, there was my father's final pastorate, a simple brick building in a mostly Jewish suburb that smelled like every church I had ever known: a little musty with a mix of cedar, peppermint, and Old Spice cologne. I would use the spare key under the welcome mat to let myself in and sit behind the piano for hours, just me and Jesus. The sun would shine in the windows at the perfect angle where you could see little dust particles floating in the light beams, and colors from the stained-glass windows made prisms on the wall.

In every church I found along the way, old or new, I was fascinated by the intricate work of stained-glass windows, each one telling a story illustrated by broken fragments of color, familiar but never the same:

> Jesus teaching,
> disciples following,
> a garden weeping,
> Pilate politicizing,
> crowds screaming,
> the cross looming,
> a crown gleaming,
> Mary mourning,
> the grave groaning,
> the King ascending,
> Jesus sending,
> heaven beaming.

These are the stories many of us heard growing up, they are the stories that captured our hearts and introduced us to a Jesus who welcomed little children, healed the sick, and provided for the poor. As much as I wish we could all hold on to the innocence of our original yes to following that Jesus, it often feels like we're children still desperate to believe in Santa Claus even after finding our parents placing the gifts under the tree. The magic disappears and our childlike faith begins to waver.

We eventually grow up and learn in every church there are rituals, traditions, sacraments, and heritage of home, but as with any house it comes with dysfunctional family members, painful memories, and hidden secrets that often go to the grave with its patriarchs. *We find drama, broken relationships, abuse, and political power grabs that match the ominous glass artistry of the betrayed Messiah and a hanging Judas.*

When Stained-Glass Windows Break

The miracle of stained-glass artwork is the intricate and intentional masterpiece that can be made from broken pieces of glass. Stories are told and re-created between the cracks, and people travel far and wide to sit awestruck and gaze upon the beauty of brokenness. What artists bring to life with these fragments is much like what our Creator does with his Church.

He makes beautiful mosaics from our collective broken pieces for his light to shine through in a darkened world. We can't help but catch the eye of even the greatest skeptic when we come together and let God use us for his glory.

God loves a good remnant.

The *Merriam-Webster Dictionary* defines a *remnant* as "a usually small part, member, or trace remaining or a small surviving group—often used in plural."[3]

"Often used in plural ..."

We aren't alone.

By biblical definition, the *Anchor Bible Dictionary* defines it as *"what is left of a community after it undergoes a catastrophe."*[4]

I can't help but think of those of us who have been part of painful church splits, confusing leadership transitions, and traumatizing exits from a position or role. It feels like a catastrophe, it looks irreparable, we look behind us at the wake of destruction and our first response is to run far away.

I have been a runner. Sometimes, I still want to run.

Yet those of us who call Jesus "Lord and Savior" are part of the "few" who will finish our race as Matthew 7:13–14 tells us: "You can enter God's Kingdom only through the narrow gate. The highway to hell is broad, and its gate is wide for the many who choose that way. But the gateway to life is very narrow and the road is difficult, and only a few ever find it."

We are part of that remnant, the small remaining quantity of not only those taking the narrow road but those who have remained in position even after disappointments and deep hurt.

Romans 11:5 reassures us that even in our brokenness God loves his remnant. "It is the same today, for a few of the people of Israel have remained faithful *because of God's grace*—his undeserved kindness in choosing them."

We are still here in our wandering, wondering, and wrestling not by our own strength but only by the grace of God.

In every church and organization, we will find brokenness. Broken men, women, families, circumstances. Broken policies, procedures, relationships. Broken hearts. Broken spirits. It isn't a matter of if, rather when, we will come face to face with this reality, and it often takes us by surprise. We look at the shattered pieces all around us and become overwhelmed by the damage. If we, those of us who have been raised in the church, don't understand what to do with it all, how can we expect a watching world to comprehend the carnage?

How could that pastor fall so blindly into an extramarital affair?

Why would God allow them to take their own life?

How come I didn't see the abuse coming?

Their marriage seemed perfect.

The ministry seemed so solid.

I did everything God asked me to do, why is everything falling apart?

If God is so good, why did he allow this to happen?

The world's response is to dismiss the Church and Christians altogether, saying things like "They are all crazy" and "I told you none of it is real." As Christ followers, as the family of God, our knee-jerk reaction may be similar as we battle anger and frustration, but I have learned anger isn't the primary emotion driving my heart. Rather, it's a deep sadness and disappointment in people I long to love and whom I have learned to trust who have fallen off a pedestal I unfairly placed them on.

Yes, I am angry, but mostly I feel deep sorrow for the person, those connected to them, and a strong conviction that we are all capable of falling. None of us are exempt from failure.

We are all one bad decision away from shattering the perfect stained-glass image others have subconsciously painted us into, not just as leaders, but as Christians.

None of us are getting out of this life without being disappointed or disappointing others.

We are all broken to a certain extent.

My first question is, *Will we allow our disappointment and disillusionment in people to deconstruct a faith we don't have the strength or support system to help us put back together?*

My next question is, *Why do we give people, especially other Christians, that much power?*

Because here's the truth: The enemy is working overtime to make sure we not only deconstruct our faith but completely destroy our relationship with Jesus and self-destruct in the process. He wants to see the Church of God implode from within, so we lose our salt and light outside the church walls.

The day my family was forced to say goodbye to the church family we loved so dearly, the enemy would have loved nothing more than for me to say goodbye to the Church and Jesus once and for all. He wants us bitter, broken, destructive, and ultimately spiritually dead so we're no longer a threat to him.

What he didn't count on was a God who knows exactly how to put broken people back together.

> We are all one bad decision away from shattering the perfect stained-glass image others have subconsciously painted us into, not just as leaders, but as Christians.

Perhaps you picked this book up and you're standing in a pile of broken glass and for lack of a better phrase, you're bleeding all over everything and everyone you encounter. A leader has failed you, the Church didn't protect you, ministry has burned you out, or a position you loved has been taken away. As someone who has been in these very places, I know the tension in wanting to remain in the pain and lick my wounds as I look for those to sympathize with and validate my hurt, while at the same time, feeling desperate for healing.

You don't have to live the rest of your life in the rubble, but healing will require daily seeking out the Healer.

Old Wounds Can Still Sting

A few Christmases ago, I got my husband a mandoline slicer. If you don't know what that is, I now refer to it as Satan's appliance. We were having some friends over for dinner and I decided it would be the perfect night to try out my husband's gift. I was about three big strokes into a zucchini when I sliced off the tip of my right ring finger. Mayhem broke out in the kitchen. There was a lot of screaming, an obscene amount of blood, and we applied pressure as we scoured Google for medical advice.

It took about three months to heal; in fact, you'd never know it happened unless I showed you the scar. I went from daily wound care to everyday chores without even thinking about it until one night while cleaning the kitchen. I hit the tip of that very finger on the edge of the counter and electric shock waves went through my hand. I was sure I was bleeding again, but when I looked down, it was just a little pink.

The wound had healed but the nerves were still tender.

I started thinking about my own ministry journey from pastor's kid to pastor and how often I've been caught off guard when an old wound still hurts. Still stings. Reopens. Even years later a comment, a look, or a miscommunication hits a familiar spot and what looks healed on the outside sends shock waves through my body.

Am I valued, am I seen, do I have an assignment, does God really have a plan, am I a good parent, am I an effective leader? All it takes is hitting an old wound up against a familiar surface to remind us we are still healing.

It's a good thing to remember. It teaches us to go slow and move with intention and walk tenderly with others as our Father walks tenderly with us. As we enter into our churches, into relationships old and new, as we take on new assignments, it's important we remember we're works in progress. We are all breathing, walking, living testimonies of God's grace.

Brennan Manning writes:

> When I get honest, I admit I am a bundle of
> paradoxes. I believe and I doubt, I hope and get

discouraged, I love and I hate, I feel bad about
feeling good, I feel guilty about not feeling guilty.
I am trusting and suspicious. I am honest and
I still play games. Aristotle said I am a rational
animal; I say I am an angel with an incredible
capacity for beer.

He continues:

> To live by grace means to acknowledge my whole
> life story, the light and the dark. In admitting my
> "shadow side" I learn who I am and what God's
> grace means. In a futile attempt to erase our past,
> we deprive the community of our healing gift. If
> we conceal our wounds out of fear and shame,
> our inner darkness can neither be illuminated
> nor become a light for others.[5]

The grace of our good Father sits with us in the broken pieces
and invites us to be part of a remnant. There is beauty in our
brokenness.

There Is Healing in the Hallway

The day before Easter in 2007 and two months before my wedding, on a cold Saturday morning in April, my dad had a heart
attack in our basement. Upon arriving at the emergency room,
we were told that my dad was not expected to survive what was
known as the "widow maker." I heard my mom and aunts crying

out to God for a miracle as I pulled back the curtain and saw my dad lying before me, lifeless. I looked at the monitors, which confirmed the bleak diagnosis, as I stood over my father and my pastor.

It felt unfair. He had dedicated his entire adult life to loving and serving people without asking for anything in return—from preaching in soup kitchens to sitting on elaborate platforms at large events, my dad was the pastor who would be on a ten-foot ladder changing light bulbs in the church foyer one minute and throwing on his Sunday morning suit the next.

I thought of all the hurt and pain he had seen through the years and couldn't help but wonder if the stress of it all had finally caught up with him.

I wrestled with God, as the enemy snarled over my shoulder, *"The Church killed your father."*

As tears streamed down my face, I battled between bitterness and intercession for what felt like hours, but it was only a few moments. My anger turned to warfare as I shifted my attention away from the accuser and onto the Healer.

I thought of every story in the Bible seared into those stained-glass windows I loved so much as a child. Blind men seeing, lame men walking, the woman at the well whose heart was broken, and a dead daughter whose father begged Jesus to call her back to life. I saw Lazarus, I saw the empty tomb, and with a guttural cry that only comes from true lament, I screamed over my father's lifeless body, "TAKE UP YOUR BED AND WALK!"

I heard a single beep and then a stampede of doctors and nurses charging toward the triage room.

Nurses came running in, the doctor pushed me outside the curtain, and I heard the electric whir of paddles as they placed them on my father's chest and shocked his heart with a single thud. My dad sat straight up on the gurney and yelled, "HEY!" and they put the wheels down and rushed him down the hall.

I remember walking in a daze toward the elevator in complete disbelief of what I had just witnessed: a miraculous healing. When the elevator doors opened, I found the hallway to his room lined with pastors, friends, and family members too many to count.

They had brought coffee and food for one another. They were making phone calls for my mom, texting other leaders, helping those from my dad's congregation get details sent out, and checking on my sister and me. There was laughing and crying and hugging, and I knew there was painful history among some of these very people now embracing in tears and relief.

There was more than physical healing happening in that hospital that day.

In the moment it wasn't about platforms, pulpits, position, policy, programming, or politics that so often tears the Church apart. We were a family. We were an army. We were a force to be reckoned with for the Kingdom of God.

I saw broken pieces come back together to create a beautiful picture of redemption.

Church hurt might be the greatest hurt of all, but reconciliation is a deadly weapon used on an enemy hell-bent on tearing us apart.

On that Saturday morning before Easter Sunday, my love for the Church was resurrected. We couldn't deny there had been hurts and wounds, but God is constantly healing us in the hallways.

He's in the secret places of inviting him into our pain; he's in the corridors of our hearts where we choose love and forgiveness over offense. The hospital hallway became a sanctuary of prayer and worship and community. I was reawakened to the beauty of God's Church in spite of her brokenness and imperfections, in spite of my own.

My need for my Church family is greater than my need to be right or to win an argument. It's greater than my need for justice or to be understood or to sing the solo everyone wants or win the war over Sunday morning bulletin fonts.

> Church hurt might be the greatest hurt of all, but reconciliation is a deadly weapon used on an enemy hell-bent on tearing us apart.

We often skip the hallway because it means awkward conversations, confessing hurtful words that have been spoken or embarrassing behaviors that caused others harm, but there is freedom in our confession.

James 5:16 says, "Confess your sins to each other and pray for each other so that you may be healed. The earnest prayer of a righteous person has great power and produces wonderful results."

I know Church hurt is real.

I know the Church has hurt many of you reading this book and you now find yourself on a spiritual gurney losing hope as the pain takes your breath and threatens to snatch the life from your spiritual body. The enemy is snarling over your shoulder, *"The Church killed you."*

Please allow me to stand over you now as I stood over my father and, with a guttural cry, scream the words, "TAKE UP YOUR BED AND WALK!"

God isn't finished with you just yet.

"You will not die; instead, you will live to tell what the Lord has done" (see Ps. 118:17).

From Hurt to Healed

My personal hallway of healing involved going to a public university and becoming a schoolteacher for several years. So when I felt ready to slowly step back into the church and ministry, I had two jobs. Gym teacher by day, worship leader by nights and weekends.

As a working mom, I felt all the guilt and tension of wanting to be home with my baby but also knowing this was part of the season. We had incredible babysitters who helped us navigate those early days, and once Annabelle became a toddler, I sent her to a little Baptist daycare down the street.

She ran that place, a baby Enneagram 3 who had a full vocabulary and an already developed social IQ. One day as I was dropping her off, there was a little boy screaming, red faced in anger and panic as his mom held back tears and ran for the exit. I was worried Annabelle would join him in solidarity, but instead she sat down next to him at the baby gate and said, "Don't worry, little boy. Mommies always come back."

From what her teacher said, she sat there with him until his face went from red to pink, his wailing turned to whimpers, and he fell asleep in sheer exhaustion.

In my twenty years of my own adult ministry, I've been both Annabelle the comforter and the panicked toddler at the gate. I've wanted to quit, I've wanted to go home, red faced and screaming, wondering if anyone recognizes I just need a nap.

Every single time I've wanted to quit, wanted to give up, God has always shown up. I can testify to this.

Our Father always shows up.

So if you're in the hallway healing with one foot in and one foot out, you aren't alone. If you're in a full-blown tantrum at the moment and everything feels lonely and confusing, if you're tired and burdened, let me be a voice of hope that God will show up here.

He doesn't abandon us in our healing process.

He isn't too far or too distant.

Just when we're about to walk away, he reminds us he carries us through it all and today that promise is true for you.

Healing might look like working a few jobs, things might not be what you thought they were going to be, and today might feel lonely. God is faithful to father us when all is good and when we're in the middle of a meltdown. He stays right with us until our faces go from red to pink, our wails turn to whimpers, and we fall asleep in his arms in complete exhaustion.

What he has called us to accomplish can wait for healing. He won't rush us through the process; rather, he will sit with us as we mourn, question, and seek out answers. He doesn't give up on us or give our assignment to someone else while he waits for our wounds to close.

Catherine Booth, cofounder of the Salvation Army, wrote:

> Whatever the particular call is, the particular sacrifice God asks you to make, the particular cross He wishes you to embrace, whatever the particular path He wants you to tread, will you rise up, and say in your heart, "Yes, Lord, I accept it; I submit, I yield, I pledge myself to walk in that path, and to follow that Voice, and to trust Thee with the consequences"? Oh! But you say, "I don't know what He will want next." No, we none of us know that, but we know we shall be safe in His hands.[6]

We are safe in his hands.

He always meets us in the hallway.

Rest in that today.

Look Up

I echo my father's advice: if you ever find yourself alone and afraid, look for the Church. Yes, she is messy and hypocritical, she is awkward and often maddening, but she is the Bride of Christ. You might find this advice odd after reading these pages so far and getting a front-row seat to how much pain the Church has caused me over the years, but what I want you to know is I'm teaching you to look up.

I'm asking you to look beyond buildings and into homes, gyms, on back roads and in alleyways. I'm suggesting we stop expecting church buildings and the people inside to meet our every expectation and instead to look for Jesus and ways to be Jesus to everyone we encounter every single day.

I'm suggesting we stop attaching a perfect Jesus to imperfect people.

And yet, at the same time, I want to remind you that God loves his imperfect Church.

Call back to remembrance the stories that came alive in those stained-glass windows and gave you hope in a Savior who would overcome the world and bring reconciliation for his Church and his children.

He sees you healing, gathering up the brokenness as he prepares to make a masterpiece out of the mess. He sees you getting out of bed when you'd rather cover your head. He hears you praying a line or two when it has felt like he was silent, he hears the lingering hope in your weary voice. He sees you hugging the necks of those who stabbed you in the back, and he has heard you speak life about those who nearly killed you. Forgiveness is so becoming on you; wear it like a fine perfume.

Others see it too, the Great Healer doing a deep work in you and on you, and those scars you carry aren't scary. They are holy.

Wear them honestly. Bare them boldly. The next great revival in God's Church won't come from those who have never been wounded; no, it will be led by those with limps and lumps who have refused to give up.

God sees you here too. Sowing seed when you'd rather be buried, still going when you'd prefer to leave, and choosing reconciliation over revenge. This healing journey is not for the faint of heart. You aren't alone, we're all being pieced back together and patched up as we run. Rest when you can, but keep your eyes on the finish line.

On the days I still want to walk away from it all, my dad often reminds me, "Natalie, keep Christ's last command your first concern."

Love God. Love people.

Remember why you said yes to Jesus in the first place. In all the chaos, in all the madness we can always find him in it. Walking on the water, parting the sea, multiplying the loaves, delivering us from our own Egypt, guiding us through every wilderness.

We haven't always been sure we'd make it back from every desert, but somehow, we found ourselves by that still water where he restores our soul for another yes, another assignment, another mission.

The Great Commission.

Why are we still here? Why do we stay? The only answer is Jesus. He's our reason, our example. He didn't quit on us.

We won't quit on him.

CHAPTER 3

GATHER THE
BROKEN PIECES

"They all ate and were satisfied, and the disciples picked up
the twelve basketfuls of broken pieces that were left over."
Matthew 14:20 NIV

It was leading worship for Campus Crusade for Christ in college
that moved me from just being a pastor's kid to finding, like the
Grinch on Christmas morning, I actually did have a heart. It was
broken, possibly even shattered, but with every conversation about
Jesus with someone who didn't know him, with every encounter in
his presence with other believers, I was learning how beautiful my
brokenness could be when combined with other broken people.

I was partnering with Jesus every single day in ministry that
felt raw, honest, and holy.

The disciples, each with their own backstory and brokenness,
joined Jesus and his message with all their humanness. Andrew,
Peter, James, and John were fishermen, and a few of them were
business owners (Matt. 4:18–22; Mark 1:16–20; Luke 5:1–11).

Thomas, Nathanael, and Philip were also thought to know their way around the sea (John 21:1–5). Matthew, also known as Levi, was a tax collector for the Roman government (Matt. 9:9–13). Simon was a zealot or politician (Matt. 10:4), and Judas was thought to be a bookkeeper who became a thief (John 12:6). These men, along with Bartholomew, Thaddaeus, and James son of Alphaeus, witnessed miracles, transformation, and revival alongside Jesus.

I imagine like any followers of a public figure today, they were eager to get one-on-one conversation with him, yet most of their time was spent being followed by large crowds as he preached and performed miracles. I'm sure even Jesus wanted a few moments of alone time, which might be why he fell sound asleep in the bottom of the boat during a storm. Jesus' ministry was only three years old when he went to the cross. The disciples most likely thought they'd spend the rest of their lives learning and serving beside him, and had they known their time would be cut short, they might have been less patient in sharing him.

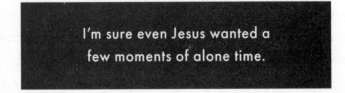

I'm sure even Jesus wanted a
few moments of alone time.

In John 6:1–14, we find Jesus and his disciples in the story of the miracle feeding of the five thousand. The disciples are finally getting a moment alone with him. In today's world this might look like being invited to watch a football game with your pastor after his Sunday morning sermon or getting to spend some time sipping coffee and sharing stories of your kids with your favorite speaker in the greenroom after her conference. There's something special about making an authentic connection with someone you admire and the opportunity to see them in their humanity.

Just as they are about to settle in for a little one-on-one time with Jesus, they notice a large crowd beginning to form around them. This same group has been following Jesus for a while now, but most of them have been more interested in the movement of Jesus, not so much the message of Jesus. Watching them slowly fill the field, Jesus casually asks one of the disciples, Philip:

> "Where can we buy bread to feed all these peo-
> ple?" He was testing Philip, for he already knew
> what he was going to do. (vv. 5–6)

Philip is about to find out.

God will disrupt our lives to test our faith.

Philip does what I would do and starts creating a business plan with Jesus. He is naming all the connections he has in the surrounding towns with bakers and bread makers, he's forming a PR campaign to raise money needed to feed all these people and a social media strategy to gain more followers to help meet the demand. After calculating cost, time, and projected growth of the crowd, he determines it would take approximately eight months for every person to get just one bite.

We do this, don't we? We get technical with God and question our resources, time, money, availability, and effectiveness of what is being asked of us. Philip was so concerned with the lack of resources around him that he forgot *the* Source was right in front of him. He failed to recognize the Bread of Life was sitting before him.

The Tale of Two Cities

One morning in November of 2016 while I was praying and journaling, I did what we all do when we get distracted, I checked Twitter. As I was mindlessly scrolling, I came across one post that intrigued me. A pastor I followed tweeted, "If you love the local church, we are hiring a worship pastor," with a link attached. Being a pastor's kid who was on my own journey to learning how to love the Church again, it pulled me in. I clicked the link, filled out the application, and by January of 2017 my family was on a plane from Cincinnati, Ohio, to Colorado Springs, Colorado, for an official interview with the pastor and church staff.

I grew up in a small suburb of Cincinnati, I went to the same high school as my mom, and in the summers I rode my bike to the pharmacy to buy candy cigarettes I'd pretend to smoke on the bridge that led to the cemetery. It was an "everybody knows your name" community where we all raised one another, and memories, too many to count, followed me from town to town. We often joked with those visiting that you could move in, but you could never leave, so when we told people we were praying about moving to Colorado, you could hear an audible gasp moving through the counties.

At the time, Tony and I had been married for ten years, we had two daughters, eight and four, my husband was excelling in his job, and I was leading worship and writing more songs than I ever had in my adult ministry. It made no sense that we would leave our families, friends, jobs, and church to move halfway across the country where we didn't know a single person or have connections.

When God wants something to happen, he will disrupt our lives to test our faith.

Just like Jesus asked Philip atop the hill in the field that day, I felt him asking me, "Natalie, what do you think about …," and all I could see was the lack, what we didn't have, and how much we were leaving behind. Our house wasn't ready to sell, our kids would have to start a new school at the end of the school year, the housing market in Colorado was triple the cost of the housing market in Ohio, and we would be leaving behind our entire extended family and nearly forty years of friendships.

Like the disciples, I was looking out over this opportunity feeling empty handed and without resources, but God was about to show me that he always makes something out of nothing.

Jesus Turns a Lunchable into a Potluck

Upon seeing a stammering Philip and the commotion of the people gathering below, another disciple, Andrew, gets involved and ultimately fails Jesus' test too by scavenging through the people. As he is going through the crowd to see what kind of food the people have on them, he eventually finds a young boy with five barley loaves and two fish.

Have you ever gone out into the world to see what they have to offer? Yeah, me too.

Now, barley wasn't exactly the meal choice of the rich, so I imagine this boy wasn't all too eager to give up what he had brought with him; he most likely didn't have a bread cave waiting for him back home. Who knows how long it took his family to save up just so he could have those five loaves and two fish? How many people witnessed Andrew asking the boy for his lunch and how many began to hide what they had in their possession?

I wonder, because of their lack of faith, how many missed out on being part of a miracle.

When this young boy handed over his lunch, he had no idea he was about to partner with the Messiah in a miracle. The moment those loaves and fish were given to Jesus, the lunch began to multiply in Jesus' hands.

What started as a little Lunchable, Jesus turned into a potluck.

What the boy and the disciples saw as just five loaves and only two fish fed every single person, and not just one bite, but every person ate until they were full.

Our God is the God of the just and only.

As the food multiplies in the hands of Jesus, he gives it to the disciples, and they are provided the opportunity to partner with Jesus in the miracle as they pass out the food to the hungry people. Even now, as you bring him what you have, he is inviting you to be part of the miracle.

He will multiply your yes.

He will add to your obedience.

I imagine it was like Christmas morning for the disciples as they watched all of those people eat until they were completely satisfied. They were *filled up*. They didn't get just one bite like

Andrew thought; they left that day full. I think one reason many of us walk away from church or ministry is because we quit before we get to this moment. We leave the field when it doesn't look like we have enough. We miss the miracle.

The Wild West

Our move to Colorado exposed my own Philip and Andrew response to Jesus. We were facing so many unknowns, a bumpy resignation from my position at my church that created fresh wounds and exposed some old ones, and I was afraid to give Jesus my family, career path, and dreams. I was afraid I was out of my league, that I wouldn't be good enough as a wife, mom, or worship leader, and we'd get out west to find famine, not favor.

It proved to be a stretching season for our entire family, and though challenging, what I found was miracle after miracle once I placed it all in God's hands.

Letting go leaves room for the miraculous.

We eventually found a beautiful home, a school for our girls with brand-new friends, a church family that became like our very own flesh and blood, and a daily reminder from the view outside my bedroom window that God speaks to and moves mountains every day on our behalf.

Have there been desert seasons? Absolutely! Have I wanted to quit a little bit of every day? You know it! Have I looked back at Ohio and longed for small-town simplicity where I'm known and loved by familiar faces? Of course!

When we moved to Colorado, I was hired to be a worship pastor. For fifteen years I had been leading worship for smaller churches and conferences, learning how to lead teams, using the latest and greatest technology, and traveling to Nashville once a month to write music. I felt ready for this new assignment and was eager to grow as a pastor, vocalist, musician, and songwriter. It was a dream job with a dream team and the church was, and continues to be, known for songwriting and creating beautiful worship projects listened to around the world.

For two years I struggled. Every Saturday before the Sunday I was scheduled to lead worship or the night before a conference or event, I became physically ill, terrified I was going to make a mistake. Compared to my teammates, I told myself I was the weak link, I was the one who couldn't follow the click perfectly or play the exact keyboard lead line or hit the note everyone needed me to hit.

In fall of 2018, a year after we made the move, I wrote in my journal, *"I'm here doing what you asked me to do and yet it feels the hardest. In a season I am being most obedient to you I feel the most pressed. You promise you won't leave me or forsake me and I'm trusting you to be my defender, but this feels like a season of punishment."*

The voices of the crowd below me had become louder than the voice of Jesus in my life. What I had grown up doing with joy and passion, leading the people of God in worship, I was now doing out of fear. I wish I could blame the enemy and say he tricked me into believing I wasn't good enough, but the truth is, I was my own enemy. Like Philip and Andrew, I was trying to partner with Jesus in ministry by pulling every worldly resource around me rather than looking to *the Source* in front of me and trusting he would multiply my yes to fill up the people he had entrusted to me.

I locked eyes with man, not Jesus.

For those of us who have been wounded by the Church, it would be easy to blame the leadership surrounding the situation. As you are reading my story, your past experiences might say, well, she wasn't set up for success or they were probably being critical or putting pressure on her to perform or they wanted someone better. Though there might be some truth weaved into those cries, what I am learning is that God will allow discomfort when he's about to work a miracle.

Sometimes what feels like failure is actually a catalyst to a miracle.

Philip and Andrew failed Jesus' test and they still got to partner with Jesus in a miracle.

Over the next several years my role shifted to preaching, teaching, and writing. Where leading worship had been my main source of communicating for most of my life, the Lord was asking me what else I had in my lunchbox. It awakened the sixteen-year-old Natalie in me who used to practice speeches in her mirror with her curling iron as a microphone, who wrote novels on college-ruled paper in her bedroom late into the night.

I can say with full confidence today that when God asks for what we have, he always multiplies it. I handed him my identity of worship leader kicking and screaming, but I knew it was better than having him pry it from my cold, dead hands. I have cried a lot, mourned lost dreams and unmet expectations, but I write this to you now in the middle of the miracle.

Following Jesus is rarely a hilltop nap listening to him tell stories as he plays a harp.

Following Jesus is more often noticing a crowd gathering below and Jesus asking, "What do you have to help feed my sheep?" and surrendering to him what we brought in our lunch.

Let's pause a moment. What are you withholding from Jesus because you're afraid it isn't enough?

Are you waking up every day with an "I'm just _____" or "I only have _____" mentality, or do you believe that your God of the just and only will multiply it until you are full and spilling over?

Though my title and role have changed over the years here in Colorado, I often lead worship as needed throughout different ministries and congregations. There are moments I still make mistakes. I feel that familiar fear rising up in me, my voice shakes and my cheeks get red, and I hear those familiar voices of inadequacy flood my head. It's in these moments I just want to walk away from worship altogether and focus on teaching and writing, things less public that I can say I'm still growing in when critiqued. I was sharing these insecurities with a fellow worship leader and friend, and she said, "Natalie, if the Lord is calling you out of worship leadership for good, then I respect your decision. But if you're quitting because you're afraid, that's something you need to take up with Jesus."

What words do you need to speak over yourself today so you can partner with Jesus in a miracle in loving and feeding his people?

God Uses Our Brokenness

The beautiful part of this particular miracle, Jesus feeding the five thousand, is this wasn't just a onetime miracle. Jesus continues to feed the people until only crumbs remain, twelve basketfuls to be exact, then he tells the disciples not to throw them away but to gather the broken pieces for later.

Like the stained-glass windows we read about earlier, God uses our broken pieces. He uses our disappointment, discouragement, and doubt to show who he is in our lives and circumstances.

Can you imagine the disciples' response to this request to pick up the crumbs? Perhaps it's much like our response when we're asked to put away all the folding chairs after a long church service or clean up spilled coffee between the pews. Maybe it's helping a neighbor gut their basement after a long day at work or picking up toys and dealing with dirty diapers after a rough day of caring for the kids.

Don't you see how hard we've worked today, Jesus?

Can't someone else clean up the mess?

But Jesus knew there was more to this miracle than they could see. He wanted to show the disciples and he wants to show us that miracles can come from our leftovers.

He met the needs of the people in the crowd that day according to *his* grace, not according to the poverty of the disciples' faith. He gave them exactly what they needed for that moment. He is giving you exactly what you need in this moment too. He is working behind the scenes to line up our miracle, but it won't be based on our faith, rather his glory (Phil. 4:19).

It's okay if you don't have the faith right now. Hear him now in this moment telling you to pick up the pieces, asking for your only, your just ... Don't lose faith. Bring him the remnant of your faith and watch him multiply it.

Keep Your Eyes on Your Own Lunch

I don't know about you, but it's easy for me to look at what other people bring to the lunch table and feel inadequate. Much like in the cafeteria in elementary school, we compare and contrast not only food selections but whose parent took the time to write a little message on the napkin. We make socioeconomic-status assumptions based off who brings generic or name-brand snacks, who uses a brown bag and who has the newest thermos. We size each other up and make assumptions before we hear a name or know a backstory.

We need to keep our eyes on our own lunch.

What God has given us is neither name brand nor generic. What he has entrusted to us is neither rich nor poor, black nor white, Democrat nor Republican. In the Kingdom of God there are no sloppy seconds, only firstfruits we bring humbly before our Father so he can multiply them for his Kingdom purpose.

The shipwrecks in our lives that we will explore together in chapter 4 often happen because we are so focused on other people and their journeys with Jesus that we start wandering without realizing we've lost our own way. How many hours a day do we spend on social media platforms comparing snapshots of strangers' lives to our own and quickly get distracted and discontent with what we have to offer?

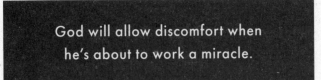

God will allow discomfort when
he's about to work a miracle.

You, reader, have exactly what you need in your lunchbox to do the very thing God is asking you to do.

Just as Andrew asked the boy for his loaves and fish, Jesus is waiting for you to give him yours. Don't miss out on partnering with God in a miracle because you're afraid it isn't enough.

Don't worry about what other people have in their hands, focus on what is in yours at this very moment. You might not have tens of thousands of followers; Jesus did his best work with twelve.

Don't throw away the broken pieces around you. Don't disregard their purpose and power. God is more than capable of taking the things that have nearly broken us to feed his people. Every rejection, every church wound, every toxic leader, every personal failure, he will use it and he will use you.

Give him your lunch. He wants to feed a multitude.

PART II

THE HARD

CHAPTER 4

SHIPWRECKS HAPPEN

"The wave of temptation may even wash you higher up upon the Rock of ages, so that you cling to it with a firmer grip than you have ever done before, and so again where sin abounds, grace will much more abound."[7]

C. H. Spurgeon

Not long ago my husband and I took our girls to the Disney California Adventure Park. They were at the perfect age and height to ride all the rides and were drawn to any attraction that spun, dropped, or went upside down. Before the trip, I had done a fair amount of research and already crossed one ride off our list: Guardians of the Galaxy—Mission: BREAKOUT!

"Do you love the feeling of your stomach in your throat as you free-fall through darkness? ... The action-packed thrill ride is sure to get your blood pumping and your heart racing.... With incredible special effects [and] thrilling free-fall drop sequences, this adventure breaks out all the big thrills!"[8]

Free-fall through darkness? Why does this feel like it should be the description of ministry before we sign on the dotted line?

81

When we first arrived at the park, we managed to keep the girls busy with all the live characters, smaller roller coasters, and attractions. As we made our way toward the Avenger Campus, we couldn't miss the giant tower looming over us. I looked at my husband, who was already green in the face, and we knew we had no choice: we were getting on the ride.

Stop the Ride, I Want to Get Off

Have you ever stood in line for a ride you've never been on surrounded by seasoned park veterans? All the "Oooooh just you waits" and little glances people give each other when they find out it's your first time aren't helpful for a nervous newbie. Once we were loaded onto the ride that consisted of a large elevator shaft with rows of seats and flimsy seat belts, I realized there was no getting off. I was committed. My girls were already lifting their arms into the air and looking for the camera that would capture the chaos. My husband was double-checking all the safety belts and bars, and I was looking into the eyes of the Disney cast member who was about to push a button that would plummet me into the depths of my greatest nightmare.

The doors closed and with a great whoosh and a blast of cold air, we were taken to the top level of the tower and dropped for what felt like an eternity, over and over. Our picture was taken at the very top as the elevator doors opened and we looked out over the entire park before free-falling all the way down. I wish you could see our faces in the professional photo we previewed as we exited the ride: a mix of terror and joy, anticipation and shock.

If we could take a picture of our journey with Jesus, the Church, and ministry, I imagine we'd get a similar result. Some of us would be captured with our arms up in the air grinning ear to ear, others holding on for dear life, some questioning their life decisions, and others staring into the camera wide eyed, silently screaming, "Stop the ride, I want to get off!"

Maybe that's where this book finds you. Your wandering and wondering have led you to this moment, standing in line for the unknown as the ministry veterans *ooh* and *ahh* and give you a few "Just you wait" comments. Now you're thinking you might have made a mistake.

Hang with me just a while longer; we're buckled in together and I'm holding on to your seat belt.

MAYDAY, MAYDAY!

The last time we heard from Paul, in our first chapter together, he was asking to get off the ride. He saw with his own eyes how deceitful and disappointing people who claim to know Christ can be and how manipulative those who call themselves ministers of the Gospel of Jesus often are in their teachings.

After following Jesus and witnessing miracle after miracle, one might assume the rest of Paul's ministry on earth would be infused with passion and zeal. Yet we find him shipwrecked and a little cynical. Can you relate?

Like Paul, I've pleaded with the Lord to take it all away, to choose someone else for this seemingly impossible assignment, and his response has been the same:

"My grace is sufficient for you, for my power is made perfect in weakness" (2 Cor. 12:9 NIV).

As carriers of the Gospel, each of us is a vessel used by God to take the Good News to the ends of the earth. This isn't limited to a church building; his ministry is wherever we, the disciples of Jesus Christ, are, serving and loving the people in front of us. Sometimes, I wish God would have installed an internal GPS into each of us to tell us where to go, complete with weather conditions and warnings of danger ahead. Because we are not hardwired with such technology, we must rely fully on the Holy Spirit, discernment, and community to help us navigate our journey. Inevitably we will experience shipwrecks that will teach us valuable lessons for our next voyage. We take the tools we have in our tool belt and set sail on an unknown course, often expecting clear skies and smooth waters.

After my twenty years of full-time ministry, shipwrecks are not unfamiliar to me. In every new assignment or relationship I expect choppy waters. Though I can't save you from your own deserted islands ahead, I can share a few of my personal shipwrecks to serve as warning flares on your journey.

Put on your life jacket, there's rough seas ahead.

The Island of Offense

We have all been shipwrecked on the Island of Offense, or will be eventually, if we choose a life of following Jesus. It is isolating, dark, and hard to see if you aren't watching for it. It's a rough terrain of dead foliage, splintered wreckage from past vessels, and inhospitable conditions that leave those left behind exposed to harsh elements. If you find yourself shipwrecked on the Island of Offense, you'll recognize those around you by their suspicion, sarcasm, and angry tweets.

Offense is a choice. We choose to take words or situations to heart and give them air to breathe, grow, and overtake our thoughts and emotions. Our immediate reaction is to fight back, to be understood, to make sure everyone knows our intentions, and this is where we lose our way.

We stop letting God fight for us.

Exodus 14:14 says, "The LORD himself will fight for you. Just stay calm." As believers of Jesus we have heard this over and over, but here's our reality: we rarely stay calm. We see the approaching storm; drama and chaos overtake us, and rather than letting the Lord steer our vessel, we take matters into our own hands and slam ourselves into the rocky shore.

We let pride drive and we put the Holy Spirit in the back of the boat.

Getting Off the Island of Offense

I believe Paul was willing to get back in the boat because he knew every voyage was moving him closer to his next assignment and finishing his race. If we don't learn from our mistakes, if we continue to get hung up on old habits and fall for the same tricks of a very unclever enemy, we won't ever have the strength or courage to step back into the boat.

If you are sea weary, I have good news for you: God is fighting for you. His presence surrounds you and he has placed in you exactly what you need to lead the people entrusted to you.

We don't pray panicked prayers or scream at the chaos. We know the Peace Speaker, the Wave Whisperer, the Storm Calmer. We don't have to spend our days cursing the wind; God has given us strategy to know exactly who our enemy is and isn't, and with great God-given authority we can move into the territories he's provided us.

Getting off the Island of Offense requires resting with confidence that no weapon formed against you will prosper. It's believing what God starts he always finishes and that includes you and me. It means resting in the bottom of the boat and letting him navigate when all you want to do is control the situation. It's trusting the battle has already been won.

Before moving on to the next island, ask yourself these two questions.

What offenses are you still holding on to?

Who are you still holding prisoner in your heart?

The Island of Self-Promotion

Up until the late 1990s, most churches and larger Christian organizations went fairly undocumented outside of a few photos placed on a website or in a local newspaper. If a church worship band released an album or a pastor wrote a book, you only knew about it through the record label or publishing house who did all the publicity. To gain access to the material, a person had to physically walk into a bookstore, music store, or shopping mall.

In the early 2000s, social media and streaming services changed the game not only for the world but for the global Church. With just one click, anyone with a computer could now find a church, pastor, worship leader, song, chord chart, sermon, or podcast. During this time, digital intellectual material came at us at lightning speed and the larger, well-known churches began representing and dominating a small fraction of the global Church, setting a standard that many other churches simply could not meet when it came to production. The smaller churches lacked the technology, volunteers, or staff to launch and maintain the programming as well as the finances to keep up with the ever-changing times.

The traditionalists, baby boomers, and Gen X, who had done most of their ministry hidden and with little resources, were suddenly seeing everything they had been missing. We were no longer satisfied with our own church homes. A friend and fellow worship leader calls this "worship pornography." The more content we view online, the less satisfied we are with the Bride entrusted to us. Rather than stay where we are and invest into that body of believers, it has become much easier to go online and look for something sexier, younger, more relevant. We break covenant with the people God had asked us to love and serve by leaving them for something more polished and most likely photoshopped.

We don't always need a storm to get shipwrecked. Sometimes we wreck because our eyes wander.

We lose vision. We covet what isn't ours. We demand another Bride.

We have created celebrities out of pastors and leaders, focusing on how many followers they have. This standard for success makes it challenging to know who is preaching Jesus and who is building a personal empire.

Even in his day Paul was trying to navigate these rough waters. We find him talking to the Corinthian Christians in 2 Corinthians 11 listing his credentials and trying to convince them that even though he wasn't rolling up in an Escalade and brand-new suit, and even though he didn't have a thriving social media following or pastor a popular megachurch, he was faithfully bringing them the *true* Gospel of Jesus Christ.

Paul promoted Jesus above anyone and anything else, including himself.

As someone who spent the first eighteen years of my life without technology, leading worship without cameras and the newest gear, who spent hours addressing and licking envelopes to send physical tape demos to recording studios in Nashville via snail mail, at times I wrestle with all of this.

How do we preach the Gospel of Jesus Christ without becoming shipwrecked as we attempt to keep up with modern-day technology, social media trends, and platforms?

Getting Off the Island of Self-Promotion

I've thought about this question a lot lately as someone who has seen the best of both worlds. I spent most of my teens and twenties pursuing a childhood dream of acting and modeling. I've been on stages, both sacred and secular. I've sought the advice of pastors and agents. I've performed in front of audiences and congregations. I've been on billboards off major highways, and I've had my name in a hand-typed bulletin seen by twenty people.

I have felt the tension of wanting to be famous and selflessly follow the Famous One. I still feel the pull of the world and what it promises, and I see how the Church struggles to fight against it while simultaneously providing greenrooms for worship leaders and promoting personalities and products.

Let me be clear for those who might be confused based off what you are hearing and seeing all around you from this culture: *The Church is not a talent agency.*

Your pastor and those in leadership over you are not talent agents.

It's vital to the Kingdom that you and I understand that it's not the job of our church or church leadership to make our dreams come true. It's when we get these mixed up that our entitlement sets in, we demand opportunity, strive to be seen, and compete for a spotlight or position that was never promised, guaranteed, or earned.

We don't need Satan to set this trap for us; we do it all on our own over time. We don't suddenly arrive on a Sunday morning or to a staff meeting demanding our name in lights; rather, it's a slow fade for some of us who feel we've earned a voice, a title, or a platform.

Perhaps it starts when we see someone else doing what we want to do. Maybe you're in an entry-level role after being a high-level volunteer with experience and tenure and it's frustrating to feel devalued or unseen. Paul is teaching us in these scriptures not to do anything for promotion or recognition, but to put our heads down and work the soil under our feet. One wilderness at a time, one shipwreck at a time.

The phone may never ring, the part may never be yours, the lights may stay dim, but God sees everything done in the secret place. He loves the secret place. If our expectation is fame, we won't recognize the beautiful roles we're given or the stories we've been woven into that are far more precious than scripts. To get off this island, to stop getting stuck, serve where you are, don't wait for a better role or a more attractive bride. Every role in the Kingdom of God is filled with adventure, holy romance, drama, and an ending that will make only one Name known.

Jesus. He is the Famous One. When we finally get to this point in ministry where we are giving people less of us and more of him, that's how we begin figuring a way off this island.

Go to Church Even When You're Not in Charge

My husband, Tony, was a professional pitcher for fifteen years. When we first started dating, I asked him if he enjoyed attending baseball games. He said, "Sometimes, but other times it feels like I'm watching my friends work."

I could relate. My whole life had been a series of waiting for Sunday, revivals, camp meetings, and assemblies where we all had assignments. Church was my job and Sunday game day. So when it came time to go to church on vacation or where we weren't in charge, it felt like I was showing up on game day to watch my friends work. I didn't know how to sit in a pew and not assess, assign, critique.

As I got older and had seasons where I wasn't on a church staff, I couldn't worship, I couldn't focus and that is when I realized how fragile my faith had become. Did I even know Jesus as anyone other than my boss? Did I see the church staff as colaborers or my coworkers? Did I love the church as my brothers and sisters or see them as consumers?

It's easy to show up and work, be productive, prove our worth, make decisions, feel important … to spend service time talking to other staff people in the lobby and greenroom. But sometimes God gives us time in his house not to clean, assign chores, do the grilling or cooking but simply sit in the living room and be ministered to by his family, in his presence and without a single task at hand.

And we don't sit there writing down ways we could do it better. We're not evaluating the house or its people. We're simply there to encounter the Father, and we have to get better at it.

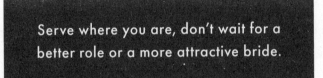

Serve where you are, don't wait for a better role or a more attractive bride.

Learning when we're not the teacher, worshipping when we're not the leader, showing up even when nobody is looking for us. It's what keeps us falling in love with the Bride he has given us and with Jesus. Some of our greatest ministry will happen in conversations in parking lots, between stalls in a bathroom, picking up our kids from children's ministry and simply as a fellow believer, not staff member or volunteer.

To get off this island we keep showing up to the House of God even when it's not ours to manage, because we're desperate for him.

We can quote the psalmist all day long with "A single day in your courts is better than a thousand anywhere else" (Ps. 84:10), but ministry has a way of finding out if we really mean it.

Want to get off this island? Make Jesus' last command your first concern.

Go and make disciples, not followers.

The Island of Lost Boys and Girls

It's not surprising we unintentionally find ourselves on this island after years of seeking a name for ourselves or expecting a perfect Bride. The Island of Lost Boys and Girls causes leaders of one generation to feel threatened by another generation and turns discipleship and collaboration instead into a perceived need to compete. What starts out as a mentorship or partnership takes a wrong turn, leaving distrust and broken relationships, and blocks generational blessing from flowing in the family of God.

I often ask the teams I lead, who is your Lois and who is your Eunice? This question is based off the scripture in 2 Timothy 1:5 where Paul told Timothy, "I am reminded of your sincere faith, a faith that dwelt first in your grandmother Lois and your mother Eunice and now, I am sure, dwells in you as well" (ESV).

Multigenerational relationships, discipleship, mentorship, and friendship, both in our biological families and church community, are what break generational curses to building new foundations of faith. This is just the beginning to staying off the Island of Lost Boys and Girls who never want to grow up for fear of losing their place at the Father's table.

Getting Off the Island of Lost Boys and Girls

The first step to getting off this God-forsaken island is to understand ministry is wherever you are as a disciple of Jesus. When I first chose the public-university route, Christian friends would say, "Wow, I'm really surprised you're not going into ministry." But they had no idea of the ministry happening all around me, through me, and growing inside of me.

They weren't there when I carried my drunk classmate to her dorm room at 3:00 a.m. and slept on her floor to make sure she was safe.

They weren't hearing the midnight conversations between my Jewish roommate and me. They didn't know how much ministry was happening as I lit the menorah with her at Hanukkah or how the presence of God filled our room as we read the Easter story together that same year.

They didn't know about the lunches with my atheist professors who wore me down as they challenged my charismatic upbringing and tried to tell me there was no God. They didn't see me wrestling with my faith and that with each day God was perfecting it.

Ministry is all around us, and if we let him, he'll show us it isn't confined to a position in a church building that we fear can be stolen. It's in the everyday hugs and phone calls we make, in teachers grading papers and doctors charting medical information, in stay-at-home moms and dads packing lunches with little notes where Jesus shows up, and the Kingdom advances because we are right where he wants us.

When we learn that ministry is right where we are, we go big, we don't hold back, and we don't wait for something better. We stop being afraid it can be stolen. We don't care if we're overlooked. It might be holding back your roommate's hair after a long night of partying or rocking a sleeping baby or mowing your neighbor's lawn. This isn't selfie material.

Setting sail with the Great Commission (go and make disciples) and the Great Commandment (love God and love people) as our North Star keeps us off the Island of Lost Boys and Girls.

Our Paul Moment

Inevitably, we will have a Paul moment. We will ask the Lord to take this thorn from our flesh and we'll ask to be let off the ride; we'll want off the boat.

There will be days we won't know if we have another shipwreck in us. It's easy to get so consumed fretting over broken bows and torn sails that we forget the indestructible Word of God is still in our hands, the irrevocable call of God is still screaming over our lives and the Great Commission is still ringing across the earth.

> Doing ministry might be holding back your roommate's hair after a long night of partying or rocking a sleeping baby or mowing your neighbor's lawn. This isn't selfie material.

This may be a shipwreck season for you now, heading one direction with the wind at your back only to be slammed against the rocks. You're collecting yourself now, taking inventory of what was lost, and it's time to map out the next adventure. This is why we keep getting back into the boat: the opportunity to boast in our weakness to reveal the strength of our God who will be made known everywhere we go.

What are some islands you seem to get stuck on again and again? Maybe they aren't any of the three I described. Maybe you keep hitting things like identity, fear of man, approval, lack of faith, unforgiveness ... we could go on and on.

Take a moment to confess to the Lord where you keep getting stuck, and write it out in a prayer. If you want, you can pray mine with me.

"Father, I confess this is a shipwreck season and I'm scared I won't ever get off the Island of _____. Show me where I'm trying to control people or situations and where you want me to surrender in my weakness to your strength. I don't want to quit. I don't want to keep getting stuck. I trust you will calm the waters around me. Reveal to me through your Word and Holy Spirit who and what I need to release so you can continue the work you began in me. Amen."

It's time to get back into the boat. You've mourned long enough.

His grace is sufficient for you.

CHAPTER 5

PITS AND PALACES

"But God stepped in and saved me
from certain death. I'm alive again!
Once more I see the light!"
Job 33:28 MSG

If Paul is our ministry colaborer in Christ showing us how to stay on course during storms and shipwrecks, Joseph is our spiritual brother teaching us how to survive the pit and thrive in the palace. He is our technicolor sibling who flaunted what his daddy gave him one time too many before his jealous brothers lost their cool and threw him into a pit.

If you have siblings, you know where this story is going. He was dancing around showing off his straight A's, MVP trophy, and talking about dreams that involved his brothers bowing to him. It went downhill for Joseph from there. He already knew he had favor with his father, and then his God-given dreams revealed favor with his heavenly Father, which some say he should've kept to himself, but we'll get to that later.

In this familiar story in Genesis 37, we get to know Joseph, Rachel's firstborn, the eleventh and favored son of Jacob. However, in verses 3–4, we get a glimpse of the family dysfunction:

> Now Israel [Jacob] loved Joseph more than any of his other sons, because he had been born to him in his old age; and he made an ornate robe for him. When his brothers saw that their father loved him more than any of them, they hated him and could not speak a kind word to him. (NIV)

Later in that same chapter we see their plot unfold and their true feelings for their brother exposed.

"They saw him from afar, and before he came near to them they conspired against him to kill him. They said to one another, 'Here comes this dreamer'" (vv. 18–19 ESV).

Modern-Day Josephs

If you aren't a modern-day Joseph yourself, you probably lead one or know one. The Church doesn't always know what to do with the Josephs, the dreamers. They aren't easy to manage in their youthful zeal and zest for life. They are the "better to ask for forgiveness than permission" people, the builders and activators who, when in a hurry, speak first and listen later with mostly good intentions. They hear from the Lord; they speak with authority. They take people on adventures through storytelling that can sometimes sound like gloating if those stories involve their current successes.

They have favor in unfavorable places with influential people, and while they know how to celebrate others, they don't shy away from celebrating what God is doing in their lives at the same time. They have their coat, their favor, their word from the Lord, and they aren't afraid to tell you all about it.

Like Joseph, maybe you've spent much of your life trying to know what to do with the voice of the Lord. For those who grew up in the church, we were given our own discernment from the Lord and were then shocked when it was misinterpreted as judgment by our peers. We know we hear from God, but we haven't always had the discipline to know how or when to share what we're hearing or seeing. I've had dreams, visions, deep-down visceral reactions to people and situations and when I tried to tell those in leadership what the Lord was showing me, I was thrown into a pit, sold off to another church where I conveniently "transitioned" into a new opportunity or position.

I want to encourage those in church leadership reading these words to listen to your Josephs, and for you Josephs to keep using your voice. None of us will get it right 100 percent of the time. Frequently, young Josephs might be emotional, scared, or immature in delivery. They might even need to be rebuked or corrected in how they are communicating if it's being done in a divisive way, but pay attention to what is behind the message. Don't dismiss them as gossips or arrogant simply because you can't see what they are learning to discern.

Joseph's dad lost years with his son because he couldn't see the jealousy of his other children. We don't want to lose spiritual sons and daughters of the House because we are embarrassed to acknowledge there's dysfunction in the family.

Timing Is Everything

To those of you who have felt wrongly accused and discarded for using your voice, the story of Joseph teaches us timing is everything. When we are new to ministry or the church or when we are spiritually and emotionally immature, we can do what Joseph did and start telling the wrong people what God is revealing to us at the wrong place at the wrong time.

Going from a pastor's kid who always had a front-row seat in the Church to a pastor who would have to find my place in a new House wasn't easy. I've made my share of mistakes. I've been arrogant, I've lacked self-awareness, I've struggled with social IQ, and I've let suspicion cloud discernment from a place of insecurity and assumption.

Being new to a church staff is like being the new kid at school, and if you were the star quarterback or homecoming queen the year before, sitting in the back of the class without a reputation or entourage can shake you to your core.

You'll grow like never before if you can endure the initiation of inside jokes, enter into longtime friendships, and take the much needed time to establish trust with those you work beside and serve. Don't spend your early days at a new place trying to impress others with all your past accomplishments or name-dropping for credibility. Only time and consistency, anointing, and God's grace can give you favor in a foreign land. In due time you'll find your lane.

Stay the course, dig in, pray for patience and wisdom, don't be in a hurry to prove yourself, just be faithful. Not everyone will like you, but you don't need to be liked, just focus on being obedient.

If you are new to a church staff or to an organization, here are five ways you can start well.

1. Take time to memorize the mission statement, vision, values, and creeds. Know the history of the church. Learn it by taking a pastor or leader to coffee, asking questions, and understanding key events that may have impacted the congregation and surrounding community.

2. Familiarize yourself with all the ministries in the church and those who lead them. Know their function, who they serve, what they offer, and how you might partner with them in the future.

3. In meetings, be a student. Learn the culture, observe team personalities, seek to understand, and speak to confirm and contribute. Be careful with criticism early on. It's hard to critique a house you haven't lived in.

4. Seek out a pastor of the same sex who has longevity with Jesus and ministry. Ask for mentorship, accountability, and community. Look for wisdom over popularity.

5. Get to know the congregation. When we love the people as we learn our position, we establish

roots that won't easily be pulled up when ministry gets hard.

When you feel like you're losing your footing, remember ...

- Love God
- Love people
- Hold the rest loosely

In my own awkward Joseph years, I made a lot of mistakes
upon entering a new church. I was quick to panic when the Lord
revealed things to me, and I had to learn that, before speaking
up, before yelling "Fire!" at leadership unable or unwilling to
acknowledge there is smoke, I needed to ask myself important
questions.

*Have I prayed and fasted about this situation or individual/
people?*

*Am I taking this information to peers who have no power to
change the circumstances? In other words, am I causing more division
through gossip or slander regarding a leader or fellow brother or sister
in Christ?*

*I keep finding myself in this familiar pit. Lord, what are you
trying to teach me?*

What is my motive in sharing what God is showing me?

It's important to understand that while our calling and purpose have not changed, and they shouldn't be hidden, there is a
way we can walk in them with maturity and with a fear of the
Lord and great humility.

> When you feel like you're losing your footing, remember: love God, love people, hold the rest loosely.

Being misunderstood, betrayed, and sold off by those who have taken offense to our lack of emotional IQ takes us to a new level of faith as we learn to live in a pit when we were expecting a palace. Sometimes God lets us be thrown into a pit not as punishment but to teach us his favor can be found in unexpected places. The story of Joseph teaches us we can trust God to orchestrate all things for his good as Romans 8:28 says, "And we know that in all things God works for the good of those who love him, who have been called according to his purpose" (NIV).

You have been called to your Father's purpose and not everyone will understand the favor you have been given in certain places, assignments, or seasons of your life. It won't make sense; it can make people feel jealous or threatened and you might find yourself pushed into a pit by your own flesh and blood. Yet there is purpose in the pit, dear Josephs. Hold on, what you're learning there will teach you everything you need to know for the palace.

When You're Pushed into a Pit

We lose a lot of Josephs in the Church because, as leaders, we don't always know how to lead them. One day they are next to us in meetings and worshipping with us every weekend and the next they have moved on to another church, assignment, or worse, completely left Jesus and their faith altogether. They got hurt by people they thought cared about them and scared by the depth of the pit.

There wasn't anyone safe enough to share their experiences with who could walk with them and teach them how to use their newfound gifts. As the family of God, as the Church, we haven't learned how to mentor the Josephs and teach them how to harness their dreams. Rather than coach them, we critique them right out the doors and into a world who will gladly accept their creativity and individuality.

So what do we do when we find ourselves thrown into a pit? We thought we had the favor of the Lord and those leading us, we read our Bibles and prayed and loved people well. We thought we were on track to finally getting to the palace and instead landed at the bottom of a cold, dark well.

If it's a pit season for you, don't panic or try to claw your way out, or worse, pull others in with you. You'll most likely be tempted to rush the process and get it over with, but it has its purpose. It's lonely, scary, and an unknown, but while in the pit you aren't missing anything God has for you, even if it sounds like the rest of the family is having a party without you. He is right there with you.

Hidden, Not Forgotten

When I began my new role at church three years ago, my office relocated down a hallway where I only saw other staff members on their way to the restroom. Even though I wasn't in trouble and I hadn't done anything wrong, I felt hidden and forgotten, like a kid put in the corner.

That office held a lot of pity parties, but I also gave myself plenty of pep talks and others stopped in to cheer me up with words of encouragement and prayer. Seminary doesn't prepare you for the moments you're forced to deal with personal insecurity while questioning your calling. Only through intimate lament with a good Father who listens intently, and with the precision of a Great Physician who works on our hearts, can we heal in these lonely places.

If you're searching for the holy in your hiddenness, or the glory in the gory of pressing in when everyone else seems to be stepping out, I have good news for you. God sees you in the secret places where sweat pours and tears stream and your knees are calloused from a posture of total surrender.

To those standing in the shadows, sitting in the pit, praying on the precipice, or fighting on the fringe: Stay in position! You aren't invisible. You are an intricate part of God's strategy, much like Joseph in God's big story. All of heaven watches your patient endurance, and your name is on the lips of your Father, even if nobody here seems to remember it. He is aware of your whereabouts.

If you are looking for the holy in your hiddenness, know that you're already standing on holy ground—even if it's the bottom of a pit. God isn't interested in your visibility as much as your availability, so don't grow weary in the waiting. His eyes are on you.

> Sometimes God lets us be thrown into a pit not as punishment but to teach us his favor can be found in unexpected places.

Isaiah 49:2 says, "He gave me speech that would cut and penetrate. He kept his hand on me to protect me. He made me his straight arrow and hid me in his quiver" (MSG).

If you are obediently serving where God has you, even in a pit you have his favor.

He is providing for you everything you need: speaking to you, giving you dreams, teaching you good things, surrounding you with people you may not have chosen but whom he has chosen for you. I pray we can learn to see the favor of the Lord right where we are, head down, eyes on him.

In 2 Corinthians 4:8–9 we read, "We are pressed on every side by troubles, but we are not crushed. We are perplexed, but not driven to despair. We are hunted down, but never abandoned by God. We get knocked down, but we are not destroyed."

The pit isn't your grave, rather the safety of a barrel where God is making new wine.

Pit Pushers

One Sunday after church I took a meal to a family who had just brought their new baby home from the hospital. I remember sitting with the mom in her living room as she fed her newest daughter, watching her five-year-old play with her barely two-year-old who was into everything around him. Without warning, the oldest son looked at his brother and with both hands shoved the little guy right to the ground as hard as he could. The commotion caused everyone to start crying, including mom and the oldest son, who was yelling, "I didn't mean to! I didn't mean to!" as I quietly let myself out the front door.

On my ride home I felt sorry for the oldest, who was most likely feeling a bit neglected with a new baby and needy middle brother in the house. Nobody was sleeping, everyone was a bit off from their normal routine, and in a moment of unbridled emotion, he hurt his brother.

I've been tired, jealous, and in need of attention. I've felt overlooked, replaced, unseen, and hungry for someone to clap at my tricks or hang my picture on the refrigerator. Someone new comes in, younger, more talented, seemingly more anointed or favored, and in an unplanned moment I shove them to the ground, once again shipwrecking myself on familiar territory.

Just because we call ourselves Christ followers doesn't mean we won't have moments where we push down a sibling. We don't always know how to celebrate success, favor, or new seasons; we translate a brother or sister getting something we want as competition and start digging ditches in our hearts. Someone may share something God is revealing to them, then we disagree or feel threatened, we don't know how to respond, so we sabotage our very own.

We might not physically push a brother or sister into a pit, but we do it in our hearts.

I might say something hateful, or I might just think horrible thoughts about someone in the shower or while driving to work, my heart growing bitter and my mind following until I find myself hoping they fail or make a mistake to remind everyone around me I still hold value.

We will never accomplish the work of the Holy Spirit with a jealous spirit ruling and reigning over our lives.

Self-Preservation Is Not a Fruit of the Spirit

If this at all resonates with you, I can assure you that you aren't alone. Our bodies are hardwired to self-preserve, for fight or flight. Should we encounter a bear on an empty trail in the mountains or find ourselves at gunpoint in a parking garage, if we are physically and emotionally healthy, we will feel survival instincts kick in to pull out the bear spray or scream for help to save ourselves.

But we forget our worldly tactics don't work in the Kingdom of God where we actually lose our lives to save our lives. Joseph's brothers may have assumed getting rid of Joseph would solve their problems, but all it did was bring their father more pain and an embarrassing exposure of their own sin toward the end of the story.

Self-preservation is not a fruit of the Spirit. Pushing a brother or sister down because we feel attacked or threatened of not receiving a pat on the back from our parents, pastors, or peers isn't how we do things in the family of God.

He gives each of us gifts and callings and authority established before we take our first breath, so stop holding your breath; what he has for you is coming. He set his table including a place with your name on it before you ever learned how to use silverware; you don't have to steal from your siblings. Children of God aren't beggars or scavengers, so pull your claws in; there's enough for everyone.

When we get scared or overwhelmed, when we feel left out or unseen or devalued or replaced, this and this alone is our strategy:

Lead with love, serve with joy, live peacefully, practice patience, show kindness, offer generosity, war with faithfulness, demonstrate gentleness, operate in self-control (Gal. 5:22–23).

As Jesus prepared for the cross, he modeled humility as King and showed love even for those who yelled "Crucify him!" as he stood before Pilate. He could have run away or hidden in the garden or chopped off the other ear of the guard, but he didn't. Though blameless, Jesus submitted to the process of a sinner's death and chose surrender over power or position.

This is our Jesus, who teaches us that laying down our lives leads to a resurrection.

Pits, Prisons, Palaces ... Oh My!

Joseph got out of the pit when he was sold into slavery to the Ishmaelites and then taken to Egypt where he was sold to Potiphar. Later put into prison, he interpreted dreams for two of the prisoners until he caught the attention of Pharaoh, who promoted him to chief administrator of Egypt.

In the palace, Joseph encountered his brothers again when a food shortage in Canaan brought the boys to Egypt to buy food. Joseph could have ignored them or made sure they saw his success despite their attempt to kill him. Instead, Joseph hid his identity and, through a series of tests and character assessments, saw the change in his brothers. He sent for his father and Jacob was reunited with his long-lost son. God planned the entire time for Joseph to be in Egypt and save his family from famine.

The pits and prisons teach us how to behave in the palace. There we learn patience, timing, and prayer. As we learn to deal with betrayal and disappointment, it gives God the opportunity to fight on our behalf. I remember my dad once saying to me, "I'm so sorry that what you thought was breakthrough fell through." How many of us can relate?

Christians use such funny language. Sometimes I wonder if we pray for things and don't even know what we're asking God to do. *Breakthrough* is one of those churchy words that sounds great while we're leading worship or preaching but holds much weight in its actual process in our spiritual lives.

I can't help but wonder how many of us have quit or thought about quitting because what we thought would be our breakthrough fell through. We got embarrassed because we asked big and left with little. We were promised a palace and got a pit.

Somewhere down the line this word was attached to something we wanted or desired, forgetting God is more concerned with our hearts than our preferences or how people perceive us. Our obedience to the Lord, our breakthrough, is not always followed by a thriving Promised Land full of milk and honey. Sometimes, like Elijah, we find ourselves sipping water by a brook, being fed by ravens. Rather than focusing on the Lord providing for our needs, we focus on where the breakthrough is coming from.

Surely breakthrough doesn't look like being fed by scavengers.

Surely breakthrough doesn't look like being thrown into a pit and sold into slavery.

My question for you is: *What if it does?* What if the pit is a reminder that God doesn't always do what we want him to do but he always does what he promises he will do?

God is in unmet expectation. He is with us in every unanswered prayer.

Sometimes what God allows to fall through leads us to our palace and closer to forgiveness, reconciliation, and vision for our future.

Don't give up. That pit may lead to a prison, but it's teaching us how to humbly serve in the palace.

Even in the palace, we will make mistakes. We will share things God shows us too soon with the wrong people, we will flaunt our favor unknowingly and have our motives questioned by those who are insecure or feel threatened. We will be put in pits by our own people. We will put our own people in pits. We will be sold out. We will sell out others. We will be tempted with sin, and we will give in if we don't have accountability and community around us.

Let me be blunt for just a moment: there is no palace without the pit. Some of us are quitting because we thought a red carpet would be rolled out for us upon our arrival to a new season or position and, instead, we found ourselves kissing the bottom of a well.

Welcome to life. Pits are part of our process. Prisons are a natural backdrop to our story. Unfavorable places are where we find the favor of the Lord and where we are taught humility to survive the palace. We will ebb and flow from pit to prison to palace our whole lives and it will feel exhausting at times. I've learned God speaks in all three places, downloading dreams and teaching us

timing as he reveals his purpose, which usually involves reconciliation, restoration, forgiveness, and family coming back together.

The favor of the Lord has nothing to do with our circumstances. How we behave in the hidden places we never asked for
reveals a lot about how we will behave before an audience, or in
Joseph's case, how he would overcome temptation when seduced
by Potiphar's wife.

Even in the palace we will face Jezebels, jealous brothers, and
our own insecurities.

Don't ask for the palace before you've survived the pit.

No Longer Slaves

As we close out this chapter, I have to ask, and be honest with
yourself: Where does this book find you? Are you reading these
words as a Joseph at the bottom of the pit, or chained in a prison
feeling betrayed and misunderstood?

Or in self-preservation, have you been pushing others into a
pit out of fear of losing control, position, and your seat at your
Father's table?

I want to encourage you to spend some time in Galatians 4
before moving on to the next chapter. Whether you find yourself
a victim or antagonist in this part of your story, your Father loves
you with an unconditional love and he has a seat just for you. I
love these words from our friend Paul writing to Jewish Christians
straying from the Lord and relying once again on the works familiar in the law of Moses:

And because we are his children, God has sent the Spirit of his Son into our hearts, prompting us to call out, "Abba, Father." Now you are no longer a slave but God's own child. And since you are his child, God has made you his heir. (Gal. 4:6–7)

Don't forget to whom you belong. There are no favorites in the family of God, only sons and daughters.

From the pit to the palace, you have a Father who will never abandon you.

CHAPTER 6

DON'T LET YOUR JUDAS KEEP YOU FROM YOUR JESUS

*"While they were eating, he said, 'I tell you
the truth, one of you will betray me.'"*

Matthew 26:21

The story of Joseph hits a few of my high-justice triggers and if you're like me, you have a justice button that is *hot*. In my early years of ministry, it was my greatest kryptonite. It was easily provoked, just dying to be pushed and it would light up like a Christmas tree on a cold December night at the mention of anyone being mistreated, misunderstood, hurt, marginalized, or cast out. I wish I could tell you after twenty years of ministry I've learned how to harness its power, but I'm still guilty of letting it get the best of me.

I feel it right now as I write this chapter, lighting up on your behalf. Without even knowing your story, I know you've picked this book up for a reason and I'm guessing it's because someone you love and trusted, who sat at your table, betrayed you and you're ready to run. You have one foot out of the church and an eye on the back door.

You love Jesus, but sometimes your Judas is so loud.

When I read the story of the Last Supper, or I see a painting or stained-glass portrayal of Jesus and the disciples around the table with Judas sitting there all smug, I want to put a giant red *X* on his face and cancel him. Why does he get to sit there? Didn't Jesus know what he had done?

Let's read Matthew 26:14–16 together:

> Then one of the Twelve—the one called Judas
> Iscariot—went to the chief priests and asked,
> "What are you willing to give me if I deliver him
> over to you?" So they counted out for him thirty
> pieces of silver. From then on Judas watched for
> an opportunity to hand him over. (NIV)

There it is, right there in black and white: Judas betraying Jesus.

In the next part of the chapter, Jesus tells the disciples what is going to happen. "And while they were eating, he said, 'Truly I tell you, one of you will betray me'" (v. 21 NIV). And Judas is just sitting there with his bread and wine like nothing is wrong while the others are questioning themselves and asking the Lord if it is them.

Then Judas has the nerve to say, "Surely you don't mean me, Rabbi." *Are you kidding me?*

I had never really paid much attention to Jesus' response to Judas but all he says is, "You have said so."

Have you ever been at a team meeting, a family dinner, or an event and you *know* someone in the room is bad news? You have documented proof, conversations tucked away in a file folder, or hard evidence, but this person is sitting there with their Starbucks and scone making people laugh while your blood boils.

Can you feel your justice button heating up? I can.

But our Jesus, in his humanity and divinity, breaks bread with the one who would betray him. He doesn't try to expose him, call him out in a moment of irrational anger, or blame him for the coming pain. Instead, he keeps his eyes on his Father, his assignment, and the Kingdom at hand. He spends that precious time before his death with his friends, those who call him teacher and friend, and he doesn't let Judas ruin the meal.

The Great Commandment, a Great Mission

> *"The Holy Spirit is profoundly committed to restoring the first commandment to first place in our lives."*[9]
>
> Linda Dillow

In his three years of ministry on earth, Jesus demonstrated what it meant to be Great Commandment and Great Commission people. He outlined it in Matthew 22:37–39 after the disciples asked, "Teacher, which is the greatest commandment in the Law?" to which he replied, "'Love the Lord your God with all your heart and with all your soul and with all your mind.' This is the first and greatest commandment. And the second is like it: 'Love your neighbor as yourself'" (NIV).

You may have heard this passage dozens of times, and memorized it front to back to win dollar-store toys from the Sunday school treasure chest, but nothing prepares us for our Judas. I am learning the very painful lesson that in order to move forward, we may have to go backward and hear something familiar from a place of real-life experience, not hypothetical role-play.

Matthew isn't the only place in the Bible Jesus talked about loving people well and staying focused on the Kingdom at hand. In Luke 6:27–30 he said, "But I say to you who are listening, love your enemies. Do good to those who hate you, bless those who curse you, pray for those who are cruel to you …"

Does anyone else have a hard time with this?

"… If anyone slaps you on one cheek, offer him the other cheek, too. If someone takes your coat, do not stop him from taking your shirt. Give to everyone who asks you, and when someone takes something that is yours, don't ask for it back" (NCV).

Let's take a moment together to unpack this. One summer night a group of teenagers broke into our car. Thankfully, there wasn't anything of value inside, but they managed to make a mess in their hurry. When I woke up to find all the contents of our glove box littered throughout the vehicle and discovered a few personal items missing, I felt so violated knowing someone had touched my belongings with ill intentions. When someone takes something from us it feels personal, and we do our best to hunt down the thief and get restitution for what was broken or stolen.

In the Church, however, it isn't necessarily an object taken from us. Rather, someone scavenging for something valuable to call their own hijacks our identity, position, role, or an opportunity. This often feels very personal, hurtful, and violating. When we fear losing something we've held close for years, or we're afraid we will be replaced or forgotten, we are likely to respond out of self-preservation and pride.

Judas was driven by power. Jesus was motivated by his mission.

Jesus wasn't focused on exposing Judas that night, trying to change his mind, or asking the disciples to take sides. Jesus was focused on finishing what he had started, enduring the cross, scorning its shame, sitting down at the right hand of the throne of God (Heb. 12:2).

It is this kind of laser focus on the Great Commandment to love God and love people and the Great Commission to go and make disciples that moves our eyes from those who have and will betray us. This is how we keep showing up in our own imperfections and serving imperfect people—knowing at any moment we could be hurt or hurt someone else.

Judas eventually exposes himself in Matthew 27 as the one who betrayed Jesus and confesses, "I have sinned ... for I have betrayed innocent blood" (v. 4 NIV). He threw the money in the temple and hung himself. Though Judas' betrayal makes me angry, it doesn't bring me joy that it cost him his life. He knew Jesus, he had heard the teachings of Jesus, at one time he had been a friend.

When someone falls, it should break our hearts.

We have to be careful not to spend so much time waiting for our Judas to fall that we lose our own life in the process. God has called us to abundant life, but I'm wondering if we're so busy trying to expose our enemy that we've lost sight of who our true enemy is and it isn't an enemy we can see. Our real enemy is a prowling lion looking for anyone he can devour, "for we wrestle not against flesh and blood, but against principalities, against powers, against the rulers of the darkness of this world, against spiritual wickedness in high places" (Eph. 6:12 KJV).

Jesus knew who his enemy was, and it wasn't Judas.

When We're Let Down by a Leader

After watching my parents go through church hurt and the impact it had on our entire family, I wanted to expose everyone involved. Thank goodness social media wasn't around at the time. I was forced to process privately in my journals, and I found therapy in drawing little devil horns and pitchforks on certain photos in the church directory.

One night I was reading the story of David and Saul in 1 Samuel 24. While on his hunt for David, an unsuspecting Saul on bathroom break was found by David alone in a cave without his army. Up to this point the relationship between these two men had been a complicated one of deep brotherhood and friendship turned adversarial and broken. Can you relate? So often in the church we all too quickly go from family to foe, one minute inseparable and on mission and the next plotting spiritual murder against one another.

When David's men saw an opportunity for David to kill Saul, they got excited and said, "This is the day of which the LORD said to you, 'Behold, I will deliver your enemy into your hand, that you may do to him as it seems good to you'" (v. 4 NKJV). They thought for sure this was their moment for vindication and surely David would finish Saul off for good.

I imagine their complete confusion when David chose not to kill him; rather, he secretly cut off the corner of Saul's robe to show he *could have* killed him. You see, what these men didn't realize was that David had his eyes up. He knew what God had promised to him: a promise to inherit the throne of Israel. Yes, Saul was a major obstacle to getting to that promise, but God had placed Saul in a position of leadership for a reason and David knew it was God who sets up kings and sets them down, not David.

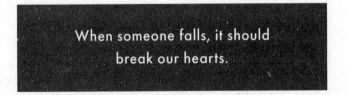

When someone falls, it should break our hearts.

Vindication, revenge, plotting, and scheming against one another won't get us to our promise any faster. God always fulfills his promises; he doesn't need our help. And even as evil as Saul had been to David, he knew the instructions "touch not God's anointed one." God would deal with Saul in his timing. This doesn't mean we can't hold leaders accountable for toxic leadership or abuse. What this means is we won't take matters into our own hands by murdering others in our hearts, with our thoughts, actions, or words.

Sometimes it means remaining quiet at the table when we want to let everyone know a betrayer is in our midst.

Sometimes it's using self-control when responding to social media posts, having someone else read a text message before we hit *send*, and choosing our words carefully to not gossip about or slander one of God's children. Yes, God loves even those who have hurt us.

I know this isn't easy; leave your Judas to Jesus, surrender your Saul.

It Is Godly to Serve Saul

> *"This truth remains: Only those you care about*
> *can hurt you. You expect more from them—after*
> *all, you've given more of yourself to them. The*
> *higher the expectations, the greater the fall."*[10]
>
> John Bevere

In our Raised to Stay community I hear the good, bad, beautiful, and broken about life in ministry and the Church. Though there are many differences in our stories of how we came to know Jesus and serve in the Church, we have one thing in common: a Saul in our lives.

I remember having lunch with a friend as I was coming out of my own cave season with my own Saul. She leaned across the table, took my hands in her hands, and in her beautiful South African accent said, "Natalie, it is godly to serve Saul." I thought of you. I thought of me. I thought of those we've lost along the way who were too wounded and exhausted to stay in position. As you're reading this chapter, you are most likely thinking of one or two people who have held authority in your life who started to change right before your eyes. Every day was a choice to show up and humbly serve and honor God's anointed one even when you struggled with honoring the person.

For some of us, it has come with great loss as we had no choice but to walk away from the people and positions we deeply loved. Sometimes honoring has meant stepping aside so the Lord can do the revealing, which I saw my own dad do with great humility and sorrow.

Other times it has meant staying to be the intercessor like a watchman on the wall and trusting God will reveal what needs to be revealed in his timing, not ours. Both approaches are equally painful. We're torn between loving someone so deeply and knowing there is something wrong, bouncing back and forth between wanting to be loyal and feeling guilty we're questioning their leadership. So, like a friend sitting across from you at lunch, let me take you by the hands now and speak these words with equal parts empathy and authority:

It is godly to serve Saul.

Serving Saul keeps us in a place of humility and reveals a dark reality that any one of us can go from being a man or woman after God's heart to leading like Saul. Remaining faithful in these most difficult seasons and serving with great love is why so many of you are still here. You've kept your eyes up, on Jesus, on your original yes and on his promises.

Giving Your Judas to Jesus

So what does it look like to give our Judas to Jesus? I'm asking myself this same question as we close out this chapter together.

My husband sent me this quote by Kris Vallotton, *"Humility is the way forward."*[11]

Ever since he shared it with me during a time I was struggling with my own Judas, serving under my own Saul, it has stuck with me. I believe the first step is recognizing we're all sinners. We all need Jesus. On any given day you and I both are one bad decision, conversation, social media post, or confrontation away from being someone's Judas. I know we all want to think we're perfect and that our intentions are good even when we unintentionally hurt someone, but the truth is, we won't get it right 100 percent of the time.

Start with prayer. Take a moment now or at some point this week to ask the Lord to show you where you have intentionally or unintentionally hurt a brother or sister. Be ready for this to be a painful process, as offense truly is the bait of Satan. When we can lay down our rights, confess our own offenses and where we may have caused offense, it takes away his power and puts the people and situations back into the hands of the Father.

Respond with humility. Perhaps you aren't in a place of leadership, but you've served under a Saul and taken your offenses to inappropriate places and "touched God's anointed one" through gossip, slander, or disrespectful behavior. Ask the Lord to forgive you for trying to take matters into your own hands. Ask him right now in the stillness of this moment to teach you how to forgive. Remember, forgiving doesn't mean trusting, it means setting ourselves free from anger and bitterness so the Lord can begin a healing work in our hearts.

Confess hurt and/or betrayal. For those who may have one foot out the door and one eye on the church door exit, don't run from

Jesus. Stay. I don't just mean in a physical church building because God knows sometimes the best thing to do is leave toxic situations or take a sabbatical or rest. I'm talking about running from the Lord. You, reader, who may have been so hurt by your Judas that they became an excuse to flee an Egypt that was meant to challenge you to grow up and not hold you captive: speak up and learn to travail.

> I know we all want to think we're perfect and that our intentions are good even when we unintentionally hurt someone, but the truth is, we won't get it right 100 percent of the time.

Just as Jesus would suffer on the cross and raise up from his grave, and just as David would step into his role as king, God has something for each of us to accomplish for his glory, but we won't see it to completion if we quit. If you'll allow me, let me sit with you in that tension right where you are in this moment. I have been hurt too. I have been wronged, talked about, betrayed, overlooked, misjudged. Jesus was too.

"In My greatest hour of need, My closest friends deserted Me. Judas betrayed Me, Peter denied Me, and the rest fled for their lives. Only John followed from afar. I had cared for them for over three years, feeding them and teaching them. Yet as I died for the sins of the world, I forgave. I released all of them—from My friends who had deserted Me to the Roman guard who had cruci-fied Me. They didn't ask for forgiveness, yet I freely gave it."[12]

I am so glad Jesus didn't run. I think all the time about how grateful I am that Jesus took on that cross for the joy set before him.

For the joy set before us.

Forgive what you can in the moment. When God makes something right, there is true restoration, healing, forgiveness, and change. God wants to free us from the chains of bitterness and unforgiveness, and it is worth every attempt to contend for forgiveness and reconciliation in the family of God. Write a letter to the person who has hurt you, or whom you have hurt, and put everything on paper that you'd want to say to them but aren't able to right now. Put it in an envelope, seal it shut, and pray over it as you give the person and situation over to the Lord. You may never send this letter, but it's a great way to name your pain rather than letting the offense become a deep wound.

It may seem like every table has a Judas, like every assignment comes with a Saul.

But your Jesus is there too.

Lock your eyes on him.

PART III

THE HOPE

CHAPTER 7

PURSUING PAUL

"Let your hopes, not your hurts, shape your future."[13]
Robert H. Schuller

Once betrayed by a friend or led astray by a leader, it becomes more challenging to welcome any voice into our lives as we make big decisions for ourselves, our family, and ministry. In his book *Managing Leadership Anxiety: Yours and Theirs*, Steve Cuss wrote:

> A couple of church pastors in your past used power to cause you pain. This is a singular truth, but your internal filter makes it universally true: now all pastors are suspect. This universal truth is reinforced by same species syndrome. The previous pain came at the hand of some church leaders; therefore, all church leaders are highly suspicious.[14]

You might be nodding your head furiously at this quote and asking the very real question, "If there is a Judas at every table, how do we know one of our friends won't turn on us? If there is a Saul in every organization, how do we trust we're being led with genuine authenticity and love?"

Our first six chapters together focused on church hurt and difficult seasons as we acknowledged we've not only been a victim but also a villain in our own story and the stories of others. Though difficult to admit, this allows us to take a new journey toward hope of restoration, reconciliation, and forgiveness. If we quit every time we get hurt or face challenging circumstances, we'll never see the glory among the gory.

After all, God is the best at making beauty from our ashes.

He is the one making all things work together for our good.

Hope in the Wreckage

I'd be remiss if, after talking so much about Paul in previous chapters, I didn't mention Timothy, a young man who joined Paul during one of his later missionary journeys. If anyone had a reason to be afraid of getting hurt, it was Timothy. Christians were being persecuted and killed for their faith under Nero, the emperor of the Roman Empire. If ever there was a time for Timothy to run and hide, to fear for his future or question God's faithfulness, it was at that very moment Paul was asking him to join his crusade.

Isn't that just like our Father? He demonstrates his power and sovereignty in our lives when we feel most vulnerable and exposed. Though young, Timothy had most likely come into contact with unhealthy leaders or witnessed poor leadership along the way. I imagine he felt both excitement and trepidation upon joining Paul, much like we might in starting a new position at our place of employment or going through oversight changes under a new leader we don't know very well.

If we had any questions about how Paul feels about Timothy, all we have to do is look at Philippians 2:20–22, where Paul addresses the people of Philippi, saying, "I have no one else like him, who will show genuine concern for your welfare. For everyone looks out for their own interests, not those of Jesus Christ. But you know that Timothy has proved himself, because as a son with his father he has served with me in the work of the gospel" (NIV).

Isn't this such a stark contrast to the relationships we just observed in chapter 6 between Judas and Jesus and David and Saul? "I have no one else like him …" The same passage in *The Message* Bible says, "I have no one quite like Timothy. He is loyal, and genuinely concerned for you. Most people around here are looking out for themselves, with little concern for the things of Jesus. But you know yourselves that Timothy's the real thing. He's been a devoted son to me as together we've delivered the Message."

There's no competition, Paul isn't afraid that Timothy will be more charismatic or take his place. Paul's Great Commission mindset keeps him from getting stranded on the Island of Lost Boys and Girls. He not only equips and empowers Timothy to preach the Gospel, but he prepares the people for his arrival with words of confidence, authority, and blessing.

In our lives, I compare it to our elementary schoolteacher choosing us to take the beloved attendance folder to the office or our pastor asking us to open the staff meeting in prayer. At an early age we understand what it means to be trusted with something special by someone we look up to and admire.

At New Life Church, our pastor Brady Boyd often reminds us that trust is earned in drops and lost in buckets. Just as our teachers quickly learned who in their class could be trusted with trips to the office without taking long detours back to the classroom, and our pastors learned who in their staff and congregation could be trusted with a mic, Timothy would have to learn to trust Paul as his leader and Paul would learn to trust Timothy as a spiritual son. This takes time, relationship, and walking through hard seasons together for that trust to be built, but it doesn't take long for that trust to be lost.

> If we quit every time we get hurt or face challenging circumstances, we'll never see the glory among the gory.

As we look a bit closer at this relationship between Paul and a much younger Timothy, I pray it renews our hope for multigenerational mentorship that is healthy and mutual, not centralized on power or position, but rather on mission and the Great Commission. I pray it reminds us that we too can find a Paul among our own wreckage.

Hollywood Wishes, Pastor Kid Dreams

I was twenty-one years old and a junior in college when I pulled out of my driveway to make it big in Hollywood. It was a foggy

May morning, and my mom was standing in her robe as my friend, fellow actor, and roommate loaded my belongings into his sports car. I had been offered a once-in-a-lifetime opportunity to spend the summer working on an iconic television series being filmed on the southeast shore. Since making the decision to attend a state university over a Christian college, I had been struggling to find my place in the church and ministry and I couldn't help but wonder if I'd find a new community and purpose in this unfamiliar arena.

Now that I'm a parent, I give my mom a lot of credit. As a young adult with a good relationship with my parents, I had given them full permission to speak into my life. Neither she nor my dad, not even my mentors, tried to stop me, even though I could tell they were less than thrilled about my decision. That morning, as we stood in the driveway to say our goodbyes, she did the church-mom thing where she hugged me tightly and aggressively whispered in my ear, "You think you know what you're doing but God is going to *mess you up*!" Then she kissed me on the cheek and told me she loved me.

During the twelve-hour drive toward my East Coast Hollywood, I was crafting a cinematic voice-over to accompany my rags-to-riches biography narrated in the voice of none other than Morgan Freeman himself. "She was just a small-town pastor's kid with big dreams who became America's sweetheart ..." I made sure to add a little Jesus in there somewhere convenient to make it "ministry" as I imagined myself in an elaborate studio giving a press conference dressed in dark sunglasses, pearls, and vintage like a modern-day Audrey Hepburn.

A few days after arriving on set and getting settled in, without warning my plans fell through and my dreams came crashing down around me. I was jobless and alone in a very expensive condo I could barely afford. That entire summer I wrestled with the Lord. I filled my journals with questions and frustration as I navigated even more rejection and struggled with identity and purpose.

Because of past trauma with leaders who did not have my best interests at heart, and fresh memories of friends who had betrayed me, I set off on this journey alone when what I needed was a Paul. I thought a change of location, a new community, and a new adventure would help heal all my hurt and pain, that I'd find my true calling, but all I found was that same hurt and pain away from those who cared for me.

I can't help but wonder how many of us are traveling alone right now and long for someone to walk beside us, pray over us, and partner with us in ministry and everyday life. We long for that brotherhood or sisterhood, but it often seems easier to go out on our own rather than get hurt all over again. The truth is, the further we get from home and the people who truly love us, the further we move away from accountability, community, and purpose.

Like Timothy, we need a Paul, but tapping into our inner Timothy will require admitting we have been hurt, acknowledging the hard and choosing to hope, to love and be loved again. It will demand a supernatural strength to move from isolation and self-preservation to a renewed joy in God-given community where we will not just survive but thrive.

You Can Go to Counseling and Still Trust Jesus

Moving from the hurt and the hard to finding hope again isn't a one-man job; we can't do it on our own. We can try, but take it from your stubborn colaborer in Christ: it rarely works.

Say this with me: Going to counseling is not absence of faith. Taking medication for anxiety or depression is not surrendering your hope for healing. God is not in competition with your counselor or intimidated by professional therapists.

We've talked a little bit about concepts surrounding deconstruction of our faith, and overall, I'm against a full deconstruction of faith if we don't have the strength and support to rebuild a relationship with Jesus. However, I am in full support of deconstructing dangerous narratives tangled over our lives that have shaped an incorrect image of a good Father and gracious God. In my opinion, I think it's important for each of us to examine what we've been taught, untangle from harmful theology and abuse, and invite the Holy Spirit to reshape our thoughts and beliefs according to the Word of God.

I remember the church Chatty Cathys talking, unaware that my young ears were tuned to their crow. They said things like, "I heard they were in counseling. I guess they just don't trust God to do a miracle." This stuck with me all through college as I battled an unhealthy relationship with food, trust issues, and fear. *If I went to counseling, did that mean I didn't trust God?*

Hear me, reader, as we sit together in this moment. In the presence of licensed professionals who understand the critical and clinical, the holy and the hard, the sacred and the science, you can find a safe place to rewrite the unhealthy narratives with biblical truths in a language you can speak to articulate your struggle. God has given men and women beautiful gifts and wisdom to help his people, not replace him as the ultimate Wonderful Counselor.

"For lack of guidance a nation falls, but victory is won through many advisers" (Prov. 11:14 NIV).

Some translations say "people" instead of "nation." Take a moment and put your name in that space. *"For lack of guidance _____ falls …"*

The word *falls* in the Greek (*naphal*) means to "fail, fall down, cast down, fall away, divide, overthrow, lay, rot, lie down, inferior, or lost." Is there a word here that resonates with you? Do you feel like in your hurt you've felt cast down, lost, or inferior by someone you trusted or a group of people who were supposed to protect you? In Proverbs 15:22 we see yet another warning, "Plans fail for lack of counsel, but with many advisers they succeed" (NIV).

In your shipwreck season, have you caused division in the Church or relationships as a way of self-preservation? Do you feel like your God-given calling is rotting away and you feel validated in overthrowing religious systems in response to pain? This proverb is reminding us that we need many advisers, not just Instagram acquaintances or those who tell us what we want to hear, but those who can help us separate the lies from the truth and help us navigate the hurt and hard.

> I am in full support of deconstructing
> dangerous narratives tangled over our
> lives that have shaped an incorrect image
> of a good Father and gracious God.

The Greek word (*rob*) for *many* or *multitude* means "abundance, great, greatness, much, plenty, many, long, or excellent." It truly takes a village of all kinds of people to help us move from the hurt and hard to the hope and holy, and I believe we will find our Paul in this group of wise counselors.

God isn't worried he will be forgotten; after all, his presence is the greatest comfort and his Word the infallible truth. We will get some bad counsel at times, but that shouldn't stop us from continuing our journey to healing as he gives us wisdom to know who to trust and when to make an appointment with a licensed counselor.

When we have walked through hurt, when we have lived through hardships and feel like we can't get out of the pit, it is okay to have Jesus *and* a counselor. Don't let old religious ways stall your journey to healing that could eventually lead you to your very own Paul. God uses men and women in all types of professions to partner with him in miracles every single day. The enemy wants us isolated, but God invites us into community and sometimes that community has a therapist, a little coffee, and a lot of Jesus.

Finding Our Paul

It was because of good counselors, pastors, and mentors that I have had the strength to continue my pursuit of my own Paul, and not just one Paul but many. When our only experiences have led us to a Judas or Saul, and we haven't had the opportunity to serve beside a Paul, the tendency is to try to make a go of it on our own. This is exactly where the enemy wants young leaders and those on the cusp of a full faith deconstruction: exposed in the middle of the road, convinced anyone trying to help is going to hurt them.

In chapter 5 we talked a bit about how discernment from the Holy Spirit helps us detect people or situations that might not be good for us. When we're healthy, discernment is a gift. When we're unhealthy and operating out of hurt or trauma, we can confuse suspicion for discernment. In his book *The Supernatural Ways of Royalty*, Kris Vallotton wrote, "Suspicion is the gift of discernment being used by the spirit of fear." He unpacked this further, "Fear clouds our convictions and distorts our discernment. When we fill our minds with negative predictions or allow our thoughts to manipulate us into thinking about all the possible destructive outcomes of our mission, we invite fear to paralyze our progress."[15]

I wonder how many of us have allowed fear of getting hurt yet again by a leader or friend to paralyze our progress in ministry, relationships, and other areas of our lives. Our Father wants us healed and whole so we can see clearly who to invite on our journey and who to politely and wisely avoid.

It was in my Hollywood summer, when I felt most alone and isolated, that God unexpectedly brought new voices and relationships into my life. I found myself a few Pauls who helped me navigate disappointment, explore fresh areas of ministry, and heal my relationship with the Church.

God is so kind in bringing us a Paul when we're too weak or stubborn to look for one on our own. These individuals will challenge us, love us, speak kindly of us, and encourage us to live in hope, not hurt or fear. If we're willing to do the hard work, healing is close behind.

When Someone Believes in You, Let Them

Over the last twenty-five years, I've come to learn that some people who have known me my entire life—from parents and grandparents to family friends and congregants in my church—have seen God's call on my life and never stopped praying for me.

The same applies to you: even when you stopped trying, even when you gave up, even when you wanted to quit, someone always believed in you. And guess what? They still do. God will reveal them.

There are even people we have yet to meet who will lock eyes with us and see Jesus first and what we do second. They will feel drawn to us and our God-given mission. They will see who God created us to be without question, even on the days we are second-guessing ourselves.

When these cheerleaders show up in our lives, we shouldn't take them for granted. We need these saints. We need these Pauls. We need their rah-rah when we feel blah-blah, but the deal is, we have to keep going and run that ball full court.

These Pauls, these spiritual godmothers and godfathers who don't come with magic wands but prophetic power, speak the Word of God to the defeat, doubt, questions, and poverty of our human souls to help us transform from orphan to child of God. Don't belittle their gift. Don't downplay their prayers.

When someone believes in you, let them. Allow trusted voices to build you up, and in return, do the same for someone else. Finding a Paul isn't about finding someone to approve of everything we do; rather, it's an invitation for a spiritual covering for where we are going.

I recommend having a Paul on each coast, that phone call you can make in the middle of the night asking for prayer. Don't be surprised if they come out of obscurity; they won't always be the loudest voice or the biggest personality in the room. They are the intercessors, the prayer warriors, the silent partners who don't have a large following but follow Jesus with great passion. Look for the humble, tested, victorious. Look for their scars and then ask them to tell their stories. Paul had so much to teach Timothy, and it was those shipwreck seasons that qualified Paul to walk Timothy through his own.

Sit with the Wise, Not the Popular

Let's be honest. By the time Timothy gets to Paul, Paul isn't exactly winning Dove Awards and selling out arenas. One might even say that Paul is past his prime, especially if one considers Paul's "prime" to be his days partnering in ministry with Jesus (Acts 9). Paul is tired. Paul is shipwrecked. Paul is about to go to prison.

According to Acts 16:1–3, Paul met Timothy while he was traveling through Lystra, Timothy's hometown. It wasn't until Paul's second missionary journey that Timothy came along and experienced firsthand the danger of taking the Gospel to the ends of the earth. He knew partnering with Paul wouldn't be a life of Cadillacs and greenrooms filled with their favorite candy. No, partnering with Paul would be a life of true sacrifice until their death.

We will be tempted to surround ourselves with those who have large followings, a lot of influence, and can help us get our own status and connections. Christians, much like students at a high school cafeteria table, tend to surround ourselves with those who look like us and sound like us while jockeying for our own seats at the head of the class. This popularity contest rarely leads to finding mature leadership in our lives, rather competition that kills community and leaves us once again skeptical and suspicious of everyone around us.

We find our Pauls by sitting with those who have survived their own wilderness, perils, and shipwrecks. We learn from their years of experience and serve with those who aren't threatened by us or afraid to hold us accountable. Pay attention to who passes through your city, church, and community, to the quiet men and women who are about their Father's business and not in the mess of other people's business.

These voices humbly whisper over our lives with great passion and confidence.

We find our Pauls by remembering where we came from and who we have become as a result of these trusted voices. Don't allow Judas or Saul to become louder than Jesus or these precious people.

Remember the Words Spoken over You

My Hollywood summer taught me there are Pauls all around me, in ministry and corporate settings. I began looking for them everywhere I lived, worked, and served. I learned what to look for in these individuals, when to pull away and when to lean in. It hasn't been a perfect journey. I have been hurt, I have been betrayed, and I have been wounded, yet with each Judas the Lord has been faithful to bring me a Paul. In her book *Godmothers*, Lisa Bevere wrote, "Look around at the grocery stores and coffee shops. Reach out to someone who looks like they are in your next season."[16]

In the winter of 2019, in my office way down the hall, I grew tired of finding a Saul at every corner and a Judas at every table. I was ready to walk away from church and leading others—the daily exhaustion of people pleasing—to try something new.

One snowy morning, in a moment of pure lament, I curled up on my office floor, tears flowing as I begged God to release me. This wasn't my first time throwing a full-blown tantrum when things were difficult. I'd had a few of these moments as a young adult: after a bad breakup, starting a new job, then becoming a mom for the first time. Life is full of "throw yourself on the floor" moments, but we have a God who loves us enough to sit beside us until we're finished with our fit.

As I was having my forty-year-old breakdown, the door opened and suddenly my own Paul was standing over me, a woman a bit older than me who had quickly become a spiritual mentor and friend. She didn't ask any questions; she didn't try to calm me down or reason with me in my hysteria. Her sequin high heels started pacing around me as she clapped her beautifully manicured hands in a Pentecostal rhythm over me, praying and warring until I was too tired to fight anymore. I just lay there as she wore a track in the carpet, praying scriptures over me and reminding me of the promises of God.

She didn't leave me there; she was patient yet persistent, calm but with a sense of urgency, empathetic yet commanding. She stood over me and spoke one sentence I'll never forget.

"Pastor Natalie, if you quit, who is going to be here to remind the rest of us why we have to stay?"

My sobs turned to quiet tears that eased to a shuddering breath and then silence. We lay together on the floor looking up at the ceiling for what felt like hours. That moment with my Paul literally picked me up off the floor and reminded me that God wasn't finished with me. Like Timothy, I still had ministry in me and didn't have to fear man or the uncertainty ahead of me. As Paul was so quick to speak over Timothy, my friend was speaking over me:

"I remember your genuine faith, for you share the faith that first filled your grandmother Lois and your mother, Eunice. And I know that same faith continues strong in you" (2 Tim. 1:5).

God's faithfulness was woven into Timothy's heritage. His faithfulness is woven into our past as well. Even if you are a first-generation Christian in your family, you can look back and see the hand of God on your own life and the lives of those you love.

Take a moment and remember the faithfulness of your God. What are key moments in your life where God showed up and showed off in a difficult season? Write them down and spend time today and this week thanking him for his protection and provision, no matter how big or small. God doesn't give up on us and he never will, no matter how far we wander or wonder, no matter how hard we wrestle with him.

In 1 Timothy 1:18–19, Paul wrote to his "true son in the faith":

> Timothy, my son, here are my instructions for you, based on the prophetic words spoken about you earlier. May they help you fight well in the Lord's battles.
> 1. CLING TO YOUR FAITH IN CHRIST, and
> 2. KEEP YOUR CONSCIENCE CLEAR.
> For some people have deliberately violated their consciences; as a result, THEIR FAITH HAS BEEN SHIPWRECKED.

This book isn't about staying in a position at a church or job. This book is about staying connected to the vine, in relationship with Jesus, who has been speaking over you since the day you were born through his Word and his people. Paul knew that Timothy would be tempted to quit or shipwreck himself on a familiar island, and he was instructing him to remember who he was and what had been spoken over him as encouragement on the days he asked the Lord to let him do something different. Paul had seen others not only walk away from their assignment but from Jesus, and he didn't want Timothy to fall into the enemy's trap.

If you've been lying on your office floor ready to quit, let me be the voice standing over you now, your very own Paul speaking life into your weary bones as I ask you to recall the prophetic words that have been spoken over you.

"If you quit, who is going to be here to remind the world they have to stay?"

What other promises of God are you clinging to right now? What are some things your parents, grandparents, friends, or perfect strangers have said to you that stirred up the gift deep inside you and reminded you of who you are in Christ?

Write them down, put them in your journal, mirror, car sun visor, anywhere you can see them so they remind you daily to get up off the floor and dust yourself off.

What is our formula?

Love God, love people. Fulfill the Great Commission. Cling to Jesus. Keep your conscience clear.

You have a purpose and calling screaming over your life.

Let the hope of Christ, not hurt from man, be your testimony.

CHAPTER 8

DECORATE YOUR OFFICE

"I always put in one controversial item. It makes people talk."[17]
Dorothy Draper

Twenty-nine years old and twelve weeks pregnant, I waited alone in the headmaster's office of a prestigious private Christian school that smelled like worn leather and my grandpa's cherry tobacco. The Ohio summer sun penetrated the large windows, and I nervously tapped my foot as sweat dripped down the middle of my back. I held a bottle of water in one hand and my résumé in the other.

I trembled as I clutched those embarrassing two sheets of paper covered with too many dates and places to count, a collection of broken fragments of failed attempts to make something of myself. Actor, personal trainer, substitute teacher, telecom sales representative, worship leader, youth pastor, aerobics instructor. It was like a game of Guess Who?, but the character was always me! Most of my friends had now been with the same company, church, or organization for close to ten years and possessed thriving 401(k)s they actually knew how to use. And here I sat on yet another interview for another job that I'd probably quit like all the rest.

That's what I did when things got hard. I quit and tried something newer, easier, shinier, better. I ran when anything got hard, confrontational, or uncomfortable. I'd learn in time that's a luxury of the privileged.

I looked up at the clock and had just about talked myself out of staying for the interview when the panel came walking in.

I started dropping papers and spilling water, apologizing, and fumbling my words. I attempted to explain and disclaim as they pulled their readers down their noses and looked over the last few years of my life.

How do you tell someone there is a calling on your life when nobody is calling?

How do you convince a highly educated group of educators that you are appointed without any opportunities or appointments?

How do you tell them this isn't your first choice, but you just need a safe place until you can get to where you're going? You can't. You just submit the broken pieces and surrender to the discomfort of the process, the pressing. The silence was terrifying, and I thought, *Is this how you get to the new wine?*

Nope. It was sweat.

Being someone who hates uncomfortable silence, I started to elaborate not so eloquently on some of the details of my employment rap sheet. Raising one hand, the headmaster interrupted me. It was so abrupt that I assumed the interview was over before it had even begun (which honestly would have been good because I had soaked through the second layer of my suit). He took a deep breath and leaned forward like a father might before a good come-to-Jesus moment, but kind, gentle, and reassuring.

He said, "Natalie, I don't see this résumé as fickle undecidedness. I see little altars that are going to eventually get you to where God wants you. If we can be one of those places on your way there, I consider that an honor."

I started crying, right there in the interview. Huge tears, snot flowing, until a man on the panel handed me his handkerchief from a very expensive suit coat to clean myself up. Maybe it was the pregnancy hormones or maybe it was because this man saw my anointing over my brokenness, but this educator pastored me more in that hour than anyone had pastored me in my twenties. I would spend four years at that school as a physical education teacher, and in that season I learned I was more than my brokenness, more than my wandering, more than my doubt and insecurities and failed attempts for longevity.

I was more than my leaps of faith that often left me with a wounded limb.

I had a name, and it was Child of God. Reader, that's your name too.

Regardless of the résumé of brokenness, doubts, and disappointments that might define our past, we have a place at the table of the Lord that he sets for us in the presence of our enemies.

We have an assignment and a race to run marked out just for us using our unique gifts and abilities.

We don't have to apologize for difficult years, challenging assignments, barren seasons, or questions of doubt. We don't have to apologize for being angry with God, mad at the church, or uncertain of our faith. They are part of our testimony and little altars that mark the beginning and ending of trying to find where we belong and what we believe. Not what our parents believed or what we were told to believe in, but our core conviction of faith in who Jesus is to us in our own lives.

Sometimes we have to take that journey on our own, and it leads us many places where we meet new characters, encounter new plot twists, take wrong turns, and hit dead ends. It's only then, in our wandering, that we find what God has spoken over us. We find that his Word, his anointing on our lives, is stronger and more powerful than our most broken moments and biggest doubts.

I look back over the last twenty years and I'm grateful for every stop, detour, question, hard conversation, wrestling match, prayer, move, transition, and assignment, because each has a story. Each scar reminds us we're healing—every failure a sweet song of redemption that has been sung over it. We aren't broken; we're called by God to go and make disciples to the very ends of the earth! You and I both have a mandate on our lives to carry out something unique for the Kingdom—and we can't quit.

As Paul spoke over the church of Philippi, I speak these words over you.

"There has never been the slightest doubt in my mind that the God who started this great work in you would keep at it and bring it to a flourishing finish on the very day Christ Jesus appears" (Phil. 1:6 MSG).

We're taking this journey together. As you come into my "office" with sweat pouring down your back, gripping a résumé and a million questions, I hope to sit across from you and remind you that you have great work that God is faithful to complete.

My guess is you picked up this book—or were given it by a friend—because you're ready to quit. You've been thinking about it, you've talked about it, maybe you've started reading books on faith deconstruction over the past few months, but this book caught your eye.

> Regardless of the résumé of brokenness, doubts, and disappointments, we have a place at the table of the Lord that he sets for us in the presence of our enemies.

Perhaps someone you trusted spoke words over you that made you feel inadequate or unworthy. Maybe you grew up in church and went through a messy divorce or started asking hard questions that made people uncomfortable, and you were made to feel unwelcomed or divisive. I imagine some of you are pastors' kids like me; some have been on a church staff, and you have been devastated by another leader or an organization. There are many of you who have spent years serving Jesus and the Church only to feel even more isolated and burned out than when you got there.

Whatever brings you here, if you come worn down, angry, confused, frustrated, tired, overwhelmed, discouraged, you are in good company. I've been there too. I hope in these pages you have met the most amazing people who have wandered, wondered, and wrestled and found a God so gracious, so forgiving, and so kind on the other side. It is my hope to introduce you to the Jesus I've come to know over the course of my wandering, a Jesus who could flip a table one minute and weep over Lazarus the next. He gets it. He gets us. And he is for us.

We can have the hard conversations; you can deconstruct and reconstruct and detangle and untangle and have doubts and second thoughts, but I won't let you quit.

Inferior Design

I wish I could tell you I've grown beyond all my insecurities and fears, but the truth is, in all my leaving, being left, and going I have never been anywhere long enough to feel settled. While I might hang a picture or two, it always felt like I was one box away from moving out and on.

Not long ago, a good friend walked into my current church office, and I noticed her glance at my unpacked keyboard in the corner and scan my empty walls. After we covered some business, she ever so casually asked me, "Do you think one reason you haven't decorated your office is because deep down you're afraid it's temporary?"

I had moved offices during the pandemic and blamed my procrastination of getting settled into my new office on working from home. In my twenty years of church ministry, I had rarely had my own space I was proud of, and when I did, I lost it for various reasons that were often painful.

Have you ever lost your office? A position you loved? A church you truly cared for?

Have you lost a relationship, a friendship, or partnership that has left you weary to unpack bags and open up your heart again?

Because putting up the pictures is the fun part. Taking them down has always meant hard transition and, wanted or not, transition brings change. Sometimes self-preservation causes us to protect ourselves in the form of leaving our office calendar set to March of 2020. It's keeping one foot in place and the other halfway out the door in case we need to run away. It's not committing to next year because we've never been in one place longer than three years.

That same week, I went to my favorite home-decorating stores, and I finally decorated my office. My friends helped me organize the walls and hang some new lights and put down a new rug, and I swear roots started growing under it the moment we put it in place.

I think all of us aspire to longevity, to know people well and to be known. Fear of getting hurt or left keeps us from hanging the pictures, trying a new church family, investing in a new small group or community.

As a new friend, I want to encourage you to find the courage to hang the pictures.

Decorate your walls.

Plant a garden.

Open your home.

Prepare your office, whatever position you hold.

Resolve to stay, invest, trust, love, forgive, be held accountable, transition, change, shift.

Taking down the pictures can be just as exciting as putting
them up when we remember God is in the tension of transition
with us.

Just remember to keep one item in view that reminds you
of where you've been and how God has brought you through.
Like Moses' staff that parted the Red Sea, Joseph's coat that led
him from a pit to a palace, a piece of a sail that reminded Paul to
keep getting back in the boat. This conversation starter will be
an opportunity for you to share with others how God has been
faithful even in the hurt and the hard and give hope to those on
the cusp of quitting.

What was meant to harm you God has worked out for your
good.

Let's give the enemy something to talk about.

The Trauma and Triage

Recently, I watched a documentary created by a former child star
on what it was like to grow up in the nineties. The actress who
played Punky Brewster, an orphan raised by a single elderly man,
commented that she was opening up her personal vault of VHS
movies and voicemails of her past to see if it was like she remembered, or if she had created false realities for survival.[18]

Those of us raised in the church during the nineties certainly
can't compare ourselves to child stars, but we do remember what
it was like to grow up together in our own evangelical Hollywood.
We lived in a glass bowl, a fast-paced life of expectations and

growing up too fast, surrounded by influential adults and peers sending us subliminal messages they weren't okay. We just didn't know it was okay not to be okay.

We all showed up to church, put on the dresses and suits, and smiled as we sang in the choir. And just as our Tinseltown counterparts were on telethons declaring "Just say no!" in the latest campaign against drugs, we were the poster children of *True Love Waits* and *I Kissed Dating Goodbye*.

It would be easy not to talk about the pressures of our past, to romanticize youth camp and retreats and revivals with what we wanted them to be, but like that actress, there's healing in opening the vault.

Because it wasn't glamorous, innocent, perfect, or even holy at times. We saw some things we can't unsee, we were exposed to confusing rituals and beliefs, and we lost people we loved physically and spiritually who couldn't keep up the religious charade. It will take going back deep into our vaults of home movies, journals, voicemails, and memories to face our past so we can step into our future healthy, whole, and on mission.

It will take Paul and Timothy relationships to learn from the trauma in our past so we can triage our future. What does that mean? It means we can take what nearly destroyed us to help others, to truly see when others are in pain, and begin leading the way we always wanted to be led. With grace, mercy, and kindness despite our bad decisions, sin, or shame.

We can advocate, counsel, pray, preach, worship as people who have been rescued and redeemed, not just as survivors, but in the fullness of who God created us to be.

We learn to decorate our offices, our testimonies, our lives with remnants of where we've been to remind our souls that God has been faithful to redeem what the enemy has tried to use to destroy us.

The first step is acknowledging the things that have wounded us and the wounds that have yet to fully heal. It's doing the hard work of counseling, learning how to be emotionally and spiritually healthy, and stepping back into a place to be led without flinching in fear we will be hurt again.

Let's unpack a few things from our vaults together.

Accountability versus Church Hurt

I'll warn you that opening the vault and pulling out spiritual keepsakes from your past can open up some old wounds, and those wounds can still sting. As you ponder returning to ministry or simply attending church for the first time in a while, you might feel hesitant to trust leaders, develop new relationships within that community, listen to wise counsel, or take correction. Like any child, or animal, who has experienced neglect, abuse, or abandonment, even a kind new presence with pure intentions can trigger PTSD or fear. You'll be tempted to self-preserve or shy away from accountability and godly correction, but with time you can learn to trust again.

When we're acting from a place of fear and suspicion, it's often hard to discern if those holding us accountable are doing so for our own good or their own power. Stay with me here, because we've most likely all experienced a little bit of both. Many of us have good reason to hold people at an arm's length, and now with so much church abuse surfacing through brave souls telling their stories, it's validated our reasoning for keeping Jesus close and people far away.

Church hurt has become a buzzword among former evangelicals on social media and is often used interchangeably with *trigger*, *abuse*, *gaslighting*, and *toxic leadership*.

The danger is that when we as Christians use these words to describe everyday discomfort in ministry, we do a disservice to those who have endured harmful church hurt, spiritual abuse, and dangerous leadership. It minimizes their impact for change and crowds out their voices, voices they aren't using for vindication or to be divisive but to help others use their voices and see leaders held accountable.

The enemy, the true author of confusion, wants the church so busy pointing fingers at one another that we lose our strategy for the real battle. We have started using the phrase *church hurt* to describe situations that weren't actually hurt at all, rather uncomfortable seasons where our discernment became masked by fear and suspicion of one another.

Let's look at a few areas that might have felt like church hurt but in reality were difficult situations that might have wounded our ego or pride.

Church hurt is not:

- Being held accountable as a leader who is overseeing others
- Being held accountable for behavior that could cause danger to someone else

- Being held accountable for divisive language or behavior or gossip toward leadership or other congregants, staff, or peers
- Being asked to sit out of leadership for a season of healing or restoration
- Being referred to counseling to aid in personal development and care while you continue to serve
- Having roles removed to better focus on family or health
- Losing a role or position to better focus on family or health

Let me be clear: how these situations are addressed matters, and I have seen people experience true church hurt through the methods these discussions were delivered. Pastors and leaders have a responsibility to handle every issue with great love and care. People should always matter more than our HR policies and procedures, and I believe part of caring for people well is having established HR policies and procedures in place.

Yet for some, we weren't abused or mistreated. We got our feelings hurt because we were corrected. We didn't like being told no or not yet. We were embarrassed by a clunky transition that made us look bad or got caught saying or doing something in a moment of weakness that we were held accountable for and, rather than grow from it, we uprooted and quit.

Leaving a church crying "church hurt!" is much easier than staying and sitting under biblical correction. It takes humility and patience and trust that many of us don't have these days. I've had to take a lot of time over the last few years and ask myself if what I experienced in the past was true church hurt or me not liking a decision, person, or situation where I was equally at fault for some of the pain.

Sometimes we have to be honest with ourselves: we were more offended and embarrassed than hurt.

Fear of the Past Haunting Our Present

While unpacking boxes in our basement, I found my mom's creepy ceramic baby doll. Shuddering, I quickly put her back in her haunted little box where she belonged and shoved her far away where she couldn't get out, should she try.

I often hear my friends say they don't want to go to church as adults because their family was so badly hurt by the church when they were kids. I've heard this same argument made against marriage by those from broken families who are hesitant to enter into the covenant in fear they, too, will end up in divorce. From generational alcoholism to a family history of disease, from our diets to how we raise our children to how we respond to conflict, we all have unique family heritages and experiences that shape who we are as adults.

We don't want our past to haunt our present. We want to make new memories, traditions, and break generational curses, not invite them into our families or adult lives.

In Haggai 2:9 we read, "The future glory of this Temple will be greater than its past glory, says the LORD of Heaven's Armies. And in this place I will bring peace." Some translations say "the latter shall be greater than the former."

This particular temple had been redecorated by Herod, who was trying to outdo Solomon's temple, some scholars believe with the intention of trying to beat a coming Messiah to the punch. Jesus would eventually show up and worship in that temple and establish not just peace but *shalom*, which meant more than just stopping war and conflict but establishing a house that was good, righteous, and holy.

Our basements might be filled with boxes of creepy dolls, old photos, ornaments, church directories, and memories of thin walls where we heard our parents weeping together over painful seasons, but God is giving us the opportunity to decorate our own house that won't be perfect or conflict-free, but good, righteous, and holy because he dwells there with us.

> Don't be afraid to say yes to loving God and loving people because of what came out of your parents' vault.

Though my parents' story and their ministry is part of who I am, it was never meant to be the end of my story or testimony. God equipped your parents and mine for their calling, just as he is equipping you and me for our own assignment and future. Don't be afraid to say yes to loving God and loving people because of what came out of your parents' vault. God has something special for you and he flips scripts all the time; he breaks generational curses and establishes new generational blessings to show us he is the one holding the pen. Be thankful for what you've learned and how you've grown and then wait in hopeful anticipation for what he plans for you.

It happened to your parents. Your story has a different ending.

We're not going anywhere.

Decorate your office.

CHAPTER 9

I'M NOT LEAVING,
I'M GOING

*"Some people are meant to stay put, and some people are
meant to go. But running is different than going. When
you're running, you spend the whole time looking over your
shoulder. To go forward, you gotta look forward."*[19]

Gretchen Anthony

We didn't have social media, cell phones or iPhone cameras when I
was growing up in the church or even after I graduated college and
reluctantly stumbled back into full-time ministry. The only people
who knew what I was doing were those in my direct care. Nobody
knew when my dad was in foreign countries baptizing people in
bathtubs and hiding in the mountains preaching the Gospel. I
didn't have cameras on me when I taught English in an orphanage
for the first time or served food at a homeless shelter. Nobody was
there to capture eight-year-old me on a rickety upright piano in a
food kitchen trying to keep up with two hundred men stomping

their feet and clapping their hands as they belted "I'll Fly Away" at 8:00 a.m. before they would eat.

The question for all of us as we navigate the demands of ministry and our relationship with Jesus and the Church is, do we understand the original assignment? Let's review. We find the last commandment given to us by Jesus when he gathered the eleven disciples on a mountain and revealed himself as they stood in both disbelief and awe. He said:

> I have been given all authority in heaven and on earth. Therefore, go and make disciples of all the nations, baptizing them in the name of the Father and the Son and the Holy Spirit. Teach these new disciples to obey all the commands I have given you. And be sure of this: I am with you always, even to the end of the age. (Matt. 28:18–20)

This call to GO, the call to fulfill the Great Commission, wasn't a publicity stunt. It was a weighty responsibility to take the Gospel to the far ends of the earth no matter the cost, and I said yes.

Not to a platform or a title or a career but a yes to Jesus. I believed in that great cloud of witnesses. I knew the goal was to hear "Well done, good and faithful servant," and the first time I saw a social media post of a worship service, and my peers became household names, I was both terrified and curious.

Would our GO be compromised? Would we be tempted to make idols of our dreams, talents, and opportunities? Would we forget the innocence of hiddenness? Would we remain teachable? Would we still go to the places least reachable?

The pandemic made me think a lot about this as I watched our platforms grow dim, events and conferences canceled, church quit running business as usual, and my ministry friends become restless.

The world has changed quickly in a short amount of time, but God has not changed, his Word has not changed, and the Great Commission has not changed. Our yes remains the same.

To go and preach the Gospel to the very ends of the earth, baptizing people in the name of the Father and of the Son and of the Holy Spirit. Even when nobody is watching. Even when nobody is going with us. Even when we feel all alone.

Even Jesus Had to Go

I often imagine what the disciples' lives looked like after Jesus ascended into heaven, each going their own way taking the Gospel to the ends of the earth. They had experienced hurt, betrayal, and hard days with Jesus and now they were stepping into a new hope as they watched Jesus transition from their earthly friend and mentor to their heavenly Father.

Throughout the New Testament we hear some of their stories and get a front-row seat to their relationships and partnerships in ministry as they shared of prison cells, voyages at sea, and other adventures both corporately and individually on their quest to preach the Gospel.

We too will have seasons that are corporate and public and others that are evangelistic, or individual. How we leave one to enter the other is important and can have a huge impact on our relationship with God, the Church, and those we serve with in ministry and everyday life. Whether on a church staff or as a volunteer, serving the people of God is a pricey privilege that demands healthy transitions as to not cause division or strife in the body of Christ.

We can go without quitting.

We can leave without causing division.

We can celebrate transition without providing all the gory details.

It is vital that church leadership have a healthy understanding of transition and how to communicate well when changes take place within a church family or staff community. No communication, even poor communication, can result in church hurt for those in transition. Protocols and procedures keep order, while responsible transparency and consistent communication honor the person in transition and those directly impacted by the change.

The narrative of why a person goes, even if they choose to leave, is best agreed on by that individual and their church's leadership, staff, and volunteers and prevents inaccurate story lines from being written by those looking to fill in the blanks.

Clunky Transitions

Conflicts in relationships, like the one between Paul and Barnabas in Acts 15:36–41, remind us that transitions are a natural part of ministry and even in the tension of transition we can love one another well. Though this transitional challenge seems awkward, as we dive deeper into context, we can extract a story line of hope that the people of God can disagree with one another, go in different directions, and stay on mission without burning down organizations or destroying one another's ministry or reputation.

Imagine you and a good friend starting a business or ministry together, and after a while, your friend suggests you hire someone you just aren't sure would be a good fit. You talk it over, maybe have a few disagreements or heated conversations, and you both realize you're growing apart. Your vision is different, the plan has changed, and after some hard conversations, prayer, and seeking wise counsel, you decide it's time to part ways.

That's exactly what happened to Paul and Barnabas. Because of this conflict, new relationships and ministry teams were formed. Amicably, yet I imagine uncomfortably, everyone went their own direction holding the same Gospel. It was time to go. This decision wouldn't just impact Paul and Barnabas but also those who would later join their ministries.

Sometimes we go to make room for someone else.

Sometimes we go because it's best for the church, organization, or our family.

Sometimes we go because our calling cannot be contained where we are.

Sometimes we go because we're burned out and need a rest.

Whatever the reason, when we are called to go, we must listen and move when the Spirit moves. When we stay out of obligation, fear, guilt, or comfort, the grace begins to lift and our favor with the Lord and man starts to wear thin. Obedience is always greater than sacrifice.

Will the transitions always be smooth? Will communication always be perfect? Will leaders always honor as they should, and will we always honor those over us as we should on our way out? No, there will be clumsy pass-offs and awkward exits. People are messy, even the best leaders won't always get it right, and this includes you and me.

However, God can use healthy conflicts and disagreements, clunky transitions, and hard conversations in his family as catalysts for change, reconciliation, and growth.

Psalm 133:3 reminds us that where there is unity, the Lord commands his blessing. We can go without leaving. We can move on without causing division. We can outgrow one assignment as God makes room for another.

Losing a Leader

For three years the disciples traveled alongside Jesus before he was crucified, resurrected, and ascended into heaven before their very eyes. They had seen and participated in miracles, laughed, cried, broke bread, and shared life, and now the eleven men most likely stood speechless at what they had just witnessed. I wonder if they were mad, sad, confused, discouraged, frustrated, or scared. What would they do? Where would they go?

If we stay in a church for any length of time, we will lose a leader. It hurts. Even when we're celebrating and wishing them well, we still feel the loss. It's even worse when we lose a leader to scandal or moral failure; we can feel betrayed or defensive if we called them friend. The most confusing departures are when we aren't quite sure what happened; we just know they aren't around anymore.

None of it feels good. I'd like to think the empty tomb and seeing Jesus alive brought the disciples great comfort, but I imagine they wanted a few more adventures together, a few more miracles, another sign or perhaps a wonder.

We see them launch out into their own ministries; their mission clear ...

Go.

Make disciples.

It's our mission too. No matter who comes and goes, rises or falls, stays or leaves, it doesn't change our God-given assignment.

The disciples didn't lose Jesus, though his ascension changed their relationship. They took what they had learned and boarded ships, sang hymns in prisons, traveled afar, and carried with them the Good News.

Jesus is our greatest advocate to the Father, the Holy Spirit, our Guide and the Word of God, our weapon against the fiery arrows of our enemy. We haven't been left; we have been anointed to proclaim the Good News to the poor, freedom for the prisoners, and recovery of sight for the blind, to set the oppressed free.

Leaders will come and go.

Jesus Christ is the same yesterday, today, and forever.

Leaving and Grieving

Leaving is a normal, natural part of life. It begins with smaller, short-term departures, such as children leaving home for school each day, and then progresses to summer camp, and years later some head off to college. Some people marry and leave and cleave to their spouse, exchanging a childhood home for a new one of their own. Some might choose a job in a new city and leave behind a hometown of memories, friendships, and family members. Whether leaving something good or toxic, it's rarely easy, but starting new is part of growing up.

Being left behind is also a painful reality of life. Whether it was a parent who left the home when we were young, losing a best friend because their mom or dad got a new job across the country, or a pastor or mentor who had to leave due to moral failure, being left by someone we love is life changing.

In addition to the actual leaving, how we find out matters as well. Whether we learn about a departure through a note, email, phone call, or we just show up one day to find an empty staff office or bedroom dresser drawers, our young hearts can be marked when we become casualties of unhealthy transitions from our home or church house.

We feel angry, and while that might be partly true, we also feel abandoned and left behind. Many of us don't realize we have trust issues until we find ourselves in a hypothetical cave, alone with our Saul and our first instinct is to get revenge. Some of us didn't know we were wounded until we took a seat near our Judas and started flipping tables.

> People are messy, even the best leaders won't always get it right, and this includes you and me.

People will leave us and many times they won't leave us with much of an explanation or an inheritance or legacy, whether we were their biological child or their Timothy. It is also true that we will leave people, for both good and noble reasons, or because we're tired and burned out. As a result, we will unintentionally hurt others.

I have taken great comfort in knowing that while leaving and being left is part of life, our God never takes his eyes off us. He tells us in Hebrews 13:5–6, "'I will never fail you. I will never abandon you.' So we can say with confidence, 'The LORD is my helper, so I will have no fear. What can mere people do to me?'"

In the first chapter I told my own story of my family leaving our church and the impact it had on me and my relationship with the Church and Jesus. That day as we stood in front of our congregation, forced to leave without any explanation, it didn't feel like we were going. It felt like we were being sent into exile for crimes we didn't commit.

We went quietly, disappearing into the night, and my dad went from pastor to used-car salesman in a matter of weeks. The truth is, no matter how well we go or how politely we leave, we won't do it perfectly. It's human for things to feel awkward, sad, disappointing, scary, and even tense. There will be mixed emotions of relief and anger, resolution, and a deep-down hope the organization or ministry fails without you. You'll have imaginary conversations in the shower pleading your case, saying things you'd love to say in person but know in reality would only make things worse.

Perhaps you've imagined what it would be like to run into those who have wronged you and what you'd say or do. Much like David when he encountered Saul in the cave, we will have the choice to confront in anger or move on with the confidence that God has a plan.

When we are forced to leave a church or a position we love because of conflict, chaos, or confusion, our first reaction will be anger and our justice button will light up as we seek to be heard, understood, and validated.

If I may, let me challenge all of us with a few questions.

Is what you're feeling true anger or deep hurt?

Are you angry or are you disappointed, wounded, sad, scared, overwhelmed, heartsick, or any other emotion that might reveal vulnerability and grief?

Are you responding to the pain of disappointment by running away from the church or Jesus to protect your heart from feeling abandoned or hurt again?

We don't have to have a full faith deconstruction to name our pain. We can wrestle with situations and people, confide in counselors and mentors, and remain in relationship with Jesus even if our relationship with the church and other Christians feels unstable.

Jesus is the only one who can make the promise to us that he will never leave us nor forsake us. He is our only living hope. If we put our trust in man, we will be let down every single time.

Our passage in Hebrews continues with, "Remember your leaders who taught you the word of God. Think of all the good that has come from their lives and follow the example of their faith. Jesus Christ is the same yesterday, today, and forever" (vv. 7–8).

On the days you feel most abandoned and most left behind by those you thought you'd be doing ministry with for the rest of your life, remember those who have been faithful and then lock your eyes on Jesus, who doesn't change or let us down.

"Whatever is good and perfect is a gift coming down to us from God our Father, who created all the lights in the heavens. He never changes or casts a shifting shadow" (James 1:17).

When It's Time to Go …

I was in the tenth grade when my parents allowed me to attend another church in our community where I stepped into ministry opportunities with my high school friends. It was a large non-denominational church that took their youth group on mission trips, served the local schools with Bible studies and after-school activities, and taught Great Commission concepts at an age we were all still navel gazing.

At the time, I think it was hard for people in my dad's congregation to understand that by attending this other church I wasn't leaving, I was going.

Sometimes on this journey of wandering, wondering, and wrestling, going can be misunderstood and look like leaving by those who feel invested in our lives. It can appear as if we're quitting. It might be perceived as abandonment, failure, or rejection when the direction God is asking us to go doesn't come with a warranty, a five-year plan, or a GPS.

Nobody can track us or describe our whereabouts. We look lost, unsure, and travel weary, but it's here in the middle of nowhere that it gets good. It's in the going that we start building and getting creative and our discomfort forces a holy maturity that comes with spiritual adolescence and growing pains. We can't hang on to our parents, we can't rely on a decade of experience or a fancy résumé or portfolio. When God takes us off course to blaze a new trail, it looks crazy and leaves people scratching their heads wondering why we'd leave the familiar for the unknown.

I guess the only answer is I'd rather be in the unknown with Jesus than in the familiar without him.

Like I told my dad at sixteen years old, I can safely sit in a pew and check boxes to make people happy, or I can go and do what I know God is asking me to do even if nobody understands it. I'm eternally grateful my dad let me go.

Sometimes we have to let each other go so we won't want to leave Jesus. By going, our faith is strengthened, our beliefs challenged, and our offenses confronted. Some of us are still here because someone let us go and wander where we found a Jesus we had always wanted to know on a deep and personal level.

We left a denomination or a position, turned down an opportunity, or said no and it wasn't easy because the people pleaser in us wanted to check all the right boxes. We were taught to shatter glass ceilings, get the promotion, climb the ladder, get on the right boards, attend the popular conferences, get in with the right crowd ... and what has it all done for us? We're tired. Competition killed our creativity; we've learned to jockey for positions rather than rest in God's promises.

When we go, when we take up our cross and let Jesus order our steps—not man—we choose abiding over striving. We choose God's best over the world's sloppy seconds.

The greatest gift we can give each other is permission to bow out, rest, wait, pray, move on.

I wonder if some of us are afraid to go into the unknown because we've worked so hard and so long to be where we are. We're afraid to lose status, our reputation, but it's all meaningless if it's not where God wants us.

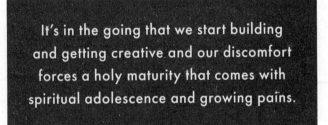

It's in the going that we start building and getting creative and our discomfort forces a holy maturity that comes with spiritual adolescence and growing pains.

I imagine both Paul and Barnabas felt like they had skin in the game with each other and the people they served. They might have felt a loyalty to stay together even though they knew it was time to part ways.

I have felt this tension before, knowing how much I've invested in a relationship or ministry and worried that if I moved on things would fall apart or people would feel left behind. Perhaps as you are reading this you are thinking back to a time you held on too long in fear of letting go, or asked someone to stick it out with you when you knew they needed to move on.

Going isn't quitting or abandoning anything. It's letting go of something that was good in order to grab hold of God's next and best. Though it's terrifying to let go, it's exhilarating to see what he has waiting on the other side of obedience.

There Is Obedience in Going

Not long ago, a good friend and mentor of mine moved with her husband and two children from Colorado Springs to North Carolina to be reunited with her estranged family. Raised by her God-fearing grandmother after she lost her mother at a young age, and having never met her father, she didn't have contact with any extended family.

Prior to her move, she received a phone call from a stranger telling her that through her son's Ancestry.com project for school they had come across her name and information. With great hope and hesitation my friend submitted professional DNA samples for herself and the other members of the family, and by the end of the month she had four sisters, another grandmother, and numerous nieces and nephews on the other side of the country.

I'll never forget our phone conversation as she told me she was going. Her voice cracked as she said, "Nat, I'm not leaving, I'm going." We wept together, prayed over each other, and mourned what we would be losing. Then we celebrated what she was gaining and how her entire legacy would be forever changed by her obedience to what the Lord was asking her to do.

Sometimes obedience is our greatest ministry to one another and our greatest weapon against an enemy of complacency and comfort.

Like in the story of Paul and Barnabas, my friend—my partner in ministry—was telling me it was time for her to go a different direction. I was so sad and disappointed because I thought we had years more of ministry together. My flesh wanted to tell her to stay, but my spirit knew it was time to divide and conquer. One God, one Word, one Great Commission. As the Church, as the family of God, we have to let each other go and send one another off publicly with kindness and words of exhortation.

I watched my friend and her husband have one-on-one meetings with our pastor, their small groups, their community, and closest friends. They sought prayer, wise counsel, and advice. Watching my own Paul pull out on this new adventure broke my heart but it strengthened my spirit. Because of her obedience it gave me confidence to make decisions of my own that tested my faith and confronted my fears.

You might rehearse a going-away speech you'll deliver with great passion to your pastor or team, heart pounding and stomach churning, but if there's one thing I've learned about going, it's God always prepares the hearts of those who love you.

Going Is Not Quitting

We will all go through seasons of transition, be it places, relationships, or jobs. It might mean we need a moment to rest, catch our breath, and regroup. But in my opinion, the church as a whole has not done a great job celebrating those called to go and pastoring those who remain, and there is a difference.

When we leave a church or a faith community, when we go to pursue new opportunities or another body of believers, why is it so hard to do it well?

Ecclesiastes 7:8 says it beautifully, "Finishing is better than starting. Patience is better than pride." This sentiment from the Bible might seem familiar because we all have one in our local church, an experienced, faithful saint who sits us down with a cup of coffee to tell us of their many mistakes and what we're saying yes to in following Jesus and serving his church.

In his *Expositions*, Alexander Maclaren wrote, "The life, which is lived for God, which is rooted in Christ, a life of self-denial, of love, of purity, of strenuous 'pressing towards the mark,' is better in its 'end' than in its 'beginning.' To such a life we are all called, and it is possible for each. May my poor words help some of us to make it ours."[20]

Many of us in ministry get excited about the beginnings: the birth of something new, the start of a fresh place and assignment. We forget that both the beginning and the end have their own purposes. How we leave affects our relationship with the church, the people we serve, and Jesus.

I want to challenge us to finish well and to go with all the authority under heaven spurring us on, leaving all our affairs in order and our office in better condition than we found it for the next person to step into.

We can't rip off Band-Aids in the Kingdom of God without some scarring. We all carry scars, and my prayer is that they aren't dreadful reminders of unresolved pain but testimonies of God's healing. Just as Paul and Barnabas demonstrated, it is possible to go and still love each other well and cheer one another on in our mission to go and make disciples.

Leaving can be done well in the family of God.

Going isn't quitting.

PART IV

THE HOLY

CHAPTER 10

I'M NOT QUITTING, I'M JUST CATCHING MY BREATH

"Do whatever it takes to catch your breath and then we'll rise up again, together."[21]

Claire Colvin

As I sat in an eclectic coffee shop in downtown Colorado Springs working on edits for this very book, I overheard a conversation. I'm not one to eavesdrop, but I was instantly drawn to their relationship, two friends having coffee who just happened to bump into each other on an unseasonably warm day in March. They casually caught up, and within five minutes their conversation went deep into their mutually conflicted relationship with the Church and Jesus: one a pastor's kid and the other raised in a local church in town.

I couldn't help myself. I got up from my round high-top, grabbed my notebook, and holding my laptop and fifth cup of coffee, awkwardly walked over to these two complete strangers. I introduced myself as a fellow pastor's kid and from there, Dana, Karl, and I connected over church-kid stories.

I explained I was writing a book and asked them if I had permission to interview them about their experiences in the church and their relationships with Jesus. The first words out of Dana's mouth were "They are letting a woman write a book?"

Dana shared she had grown up under an "umbrella of authority" where women weren't supposed to have opinions. This, along with many other rules, made her ask, "Where is the fruit of all these religious systems and black-and-white regulations?" She leaned forward, well spoken and with great passion, as she talked about her own journey from bitterness to forgiveness. Her voice strengthened as she said, "My faith is the most important thing in my life. I am learning every day what the Gospel is and who Jesus is versus what I was taught to believe he was in my life."

Karl chimed in as I asked more questions. "My personal wandering, wondering, and wrestling with the church and Jesus has actually been what made me come back and I'm more like Jesus. He's game for my questions. He can carry the weight of it all."

Karl continued:

"People can't hold the weight we're carrying; they have no space for it."

Though full of questions and past religious beliefs they were unraveling from, with every conversation and encounter with God, Dana and Karl weren't quitting Jesus. They were taking time to ask hard questions, to do the work of going to counseling, and to rewrite old scripts that had provided a false narrative of a Jesus they wanted desperately to know and love. They were resting. They were catching their breath after years of running after—and even from—religion and "being good."

And as Karl so eloquently conveyed in the quietness of that Friday morning coffee shop:

God's game for it. He can carry the weight of it all.

Resting Is Not Quitting

Together, we have navigated the hurt and the hard, and recently sat in the hope of what can come from staying to see the holy. Jesus hasn't left our side, even as we've wandered from him, and wondered and wrestled with him. You've made it, at least here with me, to this sacred space where the hurt and hard collide with the hope and holy. It's only here that we begin to surrender our offenses and painful memories and exchange them for healing and forgiveness. This is where new life can begin, new ministries can be born, and reconciliation can be found, where appropriate and necessary. We don't have to deconstruct our faith to rebuild it on a foundation of grace, love, peace, self-control, patience, and hope with Jesus and the Church.

And there's no better way to step into the holy than to take some time to rest, reflect, and respond to the Holy Spirit.

In all this talk of leaving and going, shipwrecks, and the journey from pits to palaces, one might ask, where do we rest? When do we get to take a nap? Life and ministry, even in seasons where we aren't dealing with our own Judas or Saul, when we're simply minding our own business and things are seemingly going well, are still exhausting.

The fastest way to burnout and bitterness in ministry and life is running full speed ahead 100 percent of the time out of fear that if you rest, you'll be forgotten or replaced. It's being afraid to step away from a platform or position or title because somebody might be better, younger, fresher, more charismatic. It's holding on so tightly that even on days off you're working and striving. It's refusing to go to counseling and wrestle with disbelief because we don't want to deal with years of abuse, religious webs, and other emotional baggage keeping us from running our race well.

> We don't have to deconstruct our faith to rebuild it on a foundation of grace, love, peace, self-control, patience, and hope with Jesus and the Church.

Resting isn't quitting.

But you will end up quitting if you don't rest and take time to ask the hard questions keeping you from examining your own faith and relationship with Jesus. This will require more than five minutes a morning checking your "quiet time" box to feel good about yourself. This will require time in the presence of God, getting to know his voice in the midst of all the storms and chaos surrounding you.

Remember, we aren't running this race to win. We are running to finish, and sometimes in order to finish well, we need to rest.

Jesus Took a Minute

In Mark we see a Jesus who encouraged rest, our Jesus who just needed a minute to himself as the crowds followed him witnessing miracles and listening to his teachings.

> The apostles returned to Jesus from their ministry tour and told him all they had done and taught. Then Jesus said, "Let's go off by ourselves to a quiet place and rest awhile." He said this because there were so many people coming and going that Jesus and his apostles didn't even have time to eat. (Mark 6:30–31)

The disciples were so excited to see Jesus and tell him all about the work they had been doing. Think about the first time you went on a mission trip or preached your first sermon or led your first worship set. Not everyone would understand the sheer exhaustion and exhilaration of finally stepping into your ministry or assignment, and the disciples knew Jesus would celebrate with them.

Like a good parent or friend, Jesus gave them the thumbs-up approval and then noticed their weariness. Rather than give them their next assignments, chores, or responsibilities, he made one simple suggestion. "Let's go off by ourselves to a quiet place and rest awhile."

Isn't that music to your ears? Perhaps even now you are longing for someone to give you that nod of approval and permission to rest. Even after a global pandemic where we were forced to work and learn from the comfort of our own homes, many of us are still struggling with pandemic fatigue.

Friend, you can rest.

The psalmist David wrote, "It is useless for you to work so hard from early morning until late at night, anxiously working for food to eat; for God gives rest to his loved ones" (Ps. 127:2), and again, "He lets me rest in green meadows; he leads me beside peaceful streams" (23:2).

We're all invited to those green meadows and peaceful streams where our souls are restored by a good God who isn't demanding we win a competition where he has pitted his children against one another. Rather he equips us to finish our race surrounded by a great cloud of witnesses and our very own brothers and sisters. He knew there would be days we'd want to quit even after witnessing miracles. He knew there would be years we'd question our faith and our calling, and he isn't asking us to perform or prove anything; he's showing us how to rest to get the answers we need from a Father who speaks to us.

While We Rest, Jesus Moves

In Matthew 8:24 we find a sleeping Jesus in a boat completely unphased by the giant waves and wind around him. "Suddenly, a fierce storm struck the lake, with waves breaking into the boat. But Jesus was sleeping."

Let this be a lesson to us all that we too can nap in the storm.

Like the disciples out on the rocking seas, we are more familiar with the winds and waves of life than those miracles. Even as

Jesus was walking toward them, walking on the water, it made more sense to them that they were seeing a ghost than the possibility this could be yet another miracle (Matt. 14:22–33).

Just a few verses before this moment, they had just partnered with Jesus in feeding the five thousand and watched him perform a miracle before their very eyes. Now they were in a storm, but it wasn't because they had been disobedient. Sometimes God allows the storms in our lives so he can reveal his true identity in our situations.

He will use the storms to show himself as God.

Not because we've done anything wrong, not because he's mad at us, not because he's out of control.

The seasons on the boat where God seems to be sleeping and asking us to join him in rest aren't to put us in time-out, rather to prove he is our peace speaker and we know him. He knows us.

Rest allows us to accept the storms in our lives, let God calm the seas to reveal himself, and prepare us for the next miracle.

He promised that it wouldn't be easy but that he would never leave us or forsake us. He told us that weapons might forge themselves against us, but they would not prevail.

This is an invitation to acknowledge a stormy season and a challenge to keep watching for the miracle. Expect to see people you love meet a Jesus they've always wanted to know, expect relationships to be restored. Expect God to show up and start multiplying your loaves and fish, and don't apologize for resting as you wait.

Remember, God meets our needs according to his riches and glory, not our level of faith or activity or how many people we lead to Jesus every week.

As we rest, he is walking on the water, friends. It's not a ghost. Expect a miracle.

Worry Is a Form of Meditation

As I was writing this book, I was not resting. In fact, the moment I was given this incredible opportunity to put the words God was giving me into book form, all hell broke loose. I wanted it to be a season of joy, excitement, and anticipation as I watched a lifelong dream come true before my very eyes, but instead, I was met with anxiety and the resurfacing of old wounds.

One morning I stood in my kitchen on the brink of tears and my dad came down to get a cup of coffee. He could tell I was struggling with some health concerns and fears, and after sharing a few scriptures with me, he said, "You know, Natalie, worry is a form of meditation. The enemy feeds off fear, but God thrives with your faith."

I thought about the disciples and all the times they were afraid, and how Jesus always met them and their needs according to his Word. When we meditate on the Word of God, when we remember his goodness even when we're at the end of our ever-fraying rope, he shows up and reminds us who he is over all our disappointment, frustration, and exhaustion.

He invites us to rest, to abide, in a world that has taught us to strive. When we take sabbaticals, a few weeks off from serving in our church or volunteering at an organization, or decline being the room mom at the elementary school after years of serving, it doesn't mean we're quitting. There are days, weeks, months and even seasons we need to stop and catch our breath.

God does amazing work in us while we rest.

Posture Yourself to Receive

Several years ago, a neighbor was killed tragically and senselessly. For years, every morning as we loaded into our cars for work, he would yell over at me, "Natalie, today could be the day Jesus is coming back!" and we'd look to the sky with smiles on our faces before parting ways.

I wanted to do something for his family, so our neighborhood and city rallied together and planned our very own version of an extreme home makeover.

As this massive project came closer, I would fall asleep asking God for favor with hardware stores, relationships with contractors, and for people to be generous in giving. I felt so small, so insignificant, and at the end of my own rope as I exhausted all my personal resources and contacts.

Early one morning I woke to what sounded like an audible voice in my bedroom saying the phrase "Posture yourself to receive." I jolted out of bed and did what every sane person does who hears a voice in the middle of the night ... I googled.

I typed the words "posture yourself to receive" and, after a few chiropractic links, found an old sermon from the 1980s with the exact same title.

The sermon was on the Beatitudes.

As I read through them, I realized that posturing myself to receive from the Lord, posturing myself to be his hands and feet had nothing to do with *doing* anything but confessing my full dependency on him. Casting my cares on him, resting in him. I read Matthew 5:3, "You're blessed when you're at the end of your rope. With less of you there is more of God and his rule" (MSG).

Then the next verse, "You're blessed when you feel you've lost what is most dear to you. Only then can you be embraced by the One most dear to you."

"You're blessed when you're content with just who you are—no more, no less. That's the moment you find yourselves proud owners of everything that can't be bought."

"You're blessed when you care. At the moment of being 'care-full,' you find yourselves cared for."

I lay there in the early morning sunrise postured to receive from the Lord. Exhausted, sad, heartbroken, angry, but filled with his presence and grace.

Blessed are you at the end of your rope.

Blessed are those wandering, wondering, and wrestling.

Blessed are those asking God big questions.

Blessed are those who are seeking counseling as they unravel from religious garbage.

Blessed are those who are learning how to forgive.

This is a beautiful place to be.

This is where we find our God.

Passionate Rest

Maybe you're in a season like my new friends Dana and Karl. Your wandering, wondering, and wrestling have led you to coffee shops, cities, brand-new countries, and relationships where you have encountered a Jesus who meets you in the middle of the storm and you're being reintroduced to this good Father. It would be tempting to stay in this sweet spot and grow comfortable in the rest, but this is where we are reminded to stir up the gifts of God within us that, along with his grace, enable us to get out of the boat and trust we won't drown.

It might feel scary to trust again, to walk back into a church that hurt you or even church in general after taking some time off. After several years in college attending church off and on, it was a huge leap of faith for me to take a position as a youth ministry intern at a local church following graduation. For four years I had rested, not committed to leadership roles or titles or under any religious structures or official church authority, and I was terrified I'd be hurt again.

That season of rest, that season of catching my breath and healing reminded me I still had a calling on my life that I couldn't escape. Though I was hesitant to trust people again, I had learned I could trust Jesus. He had proven to be a good friend to me, a presence of comfort and wisdom. He had provided me with good mentors and relationships that had helped me grow and mature and truly know how to study his Word.

I had found the Jesus I had always wanted to know.

Not everyone will step into full-time ministry. Some will go on to bring this Jesus into education, the medical field, politics, to their families, but it's in the passionate rest that we are reminded God has never taken his eyes off us. He has always believed in the work he began in us. He has always loved us with an unconditional love that never runs out.

Wherever you are on your journey, from resting to full-on running, you are going to be okay.

You are going to be more than okay.

Maybe you have wandered into this book fresh off a fall. Like a little kid who has crashed your bike, you just needed a rest. After a juice box and an episode of *SpongeBob*, you are ready to get back on and fly down hills with your feet raised over the pedals, the wind at your back.

Because, brothers and sisters, this is a wild ride and falling does not mean you have failed.

It's bumpy, clunky, an uphill climb to get to an exhilarating free fall, and even as your stomach is turning and churning, you know you are right where you belong. You aren't meant to simply survive this journey with Jesus, you are meant to thrive.

Sometimes that means taking a really hard fall, learning how to get some first aid, and then running right back to the place you hit the concrete. There is beauty in the blacktop, a familiar smell of both heartache and redemption in the asphalt. Sometimes we just need a fellow friend or mentor or grandmother to grab us by the face and tell us we're going to be okay.

> That season of rest reminded me I still had a calling on my life. Though I was hesitant to trust people again, I had learned I could trust Jesus.

Whatever has tripped you up, whatever skinned your knee or knocked the wind out of you, take a moment and catch your breath. You aren't quitting, you just need a moment to regroup, and God is sitting there with you.

In the quiet of this moment, ask the Lord to show you where you've been knocked down. Pray this prayer with me:

"God, I know you say you never leave us or forsake us. I know you tell me that I can rest and bring you the heavy things that weigh me down. Show me the situations in my life where I was knocked down. Show me where I've been hurt or let down and how I can confess my disappointment and frustration so you can begin a healing work in my life. Show me where I need to forgive. Show me where I need to seek wisdom or counseling. Reveal wounds I thought were healed but are still painful. I want to finish the work you started in me. Help me to get back up; help me to keep my eyes locked on you and to not be afraid."

There are so many people cheering you on and you have a good Father holding on to the back of your seat.

Take a nap, catch your breath, and then get back out there.

Your God-appointed assignment will still be there when you wake up.

CHAPTER 11

CANCEL THE QUITTING CULTURE

"I have fought the good fight, I have finished the race, and I have remained faithful."

2 Timothy 4:7

My oldest daughter started playing volleyball at a young age and joined her first travel team when she was just nine years old. Those early mornings sitting in the bleachers watching these new athletes figure out the game were painful as they struggled with coordination, strategy, and confidence. As a parent, the most frustrating part was observing kids mentally and physically give up after they missed a serve or botched a play. You could see their entire countenance change from determination to defeat, and many times they would sacrifice the rest of the day pouting in position while their parents tried every trick in the book to reengage them. Sure, they were still on the court, but they had mentally checked out of the game.

As I have observed volleyball games on the road over the years, I've come to realize it isn't just my daughter's team, the game of volleyball, or sports in general. Much like these young athletes walking off the court in tears because they made a mistake or their team made collective errors, I am afraid our current culture is making it too easy to walk out of our marriages, jobs, leadership roles, pastoral positions, and relationships without attempting to receive coaching, mentorship, counseling, or spiritual direction.

I have to ask the question:

Have we become a culture who would rather quit than fail?

Running Our Race to Win

The apostle Paul knew what it felt like to want to quit, acknowledging in 2 Corinthians 12:7, "I was given the gift of a handicap to keep me in constant touch with my limitations. Satan's angel did his best to get me down; what he in fact did was push me to my knees" (MSG).

If shipwrecks, deserts, and the wilderness weren't enough to detour him, one might assume prison and threat of a painful death might cause him to tap out. However, Paul didn't quit the game. Instead, he went on in this same passage to say, "No danger then of walking around high and mighty! At first I didn't think of it as a gift, and begged God to remove it. Three times I did that, and then he told me, 'My grace is enough; it's all you need. My strength comes into its own in your weakness'" (vv. 8–9 MSG).

Perhaps right now you feel as if you're running with a limp, fighting an enemy who can see you but you can't discern his next move. Like Paul, maybe you are just now identifying handicaps that might prevent you from finishing your race, a race God wants you to win, not abandon. Paul finished his thought here in chapter 12:

> Once I heard that, I was glad to let it happen. I quit focusing on the handicap and began appreciating the gift. It was a case of Christ's strength moving in on my weakness. Now I take limitations in stride, and with good cheer, these limitations that cut me down to size—
> Abuse.
> Accidents.
> Opposition.
> Bad breaks.
> I just let Christ take over! And so, the weaker I get, the stronger I become. (vv. 9–10 MSG)

I love Paul's transparency here. He named his limitations and laid them all out on the table. *Abuse, accidents, opposition, bad breaks*, and yet Paul was about to show us all how to finish a race to win.

Holy Hurdles

What are some of your own roadblocks or hurdles that keep you from not just winning the race but finishing? Take a moment with the Lord and confess those limitations to your heavenly Father. Write them down in the margins, a journal, or your Bible and ask him to use those very weaknesses to reveal his power in your life.

Here are a few of mine; feel free to circle a few we might have in common.

Insecurity	Fear	Anxiety
People Pleasing	Perfection	Acceptance
Failure	Inadequacy	Comparison
Church Hurt	Lack of Trust	Abuse
Betrayal	My Past	Identity

When I look at this list, I'm tempted to feel embarrassed. The enemy is quick to condemn me with the lie, "If you really loved God and were a real Christian, you wouldn't have these struggles." Don't believe it! Like Paul, we can look at our list and let Christ take over. The weaker we get, the stronger he becomes.

Of course, God wants us to finish our race, but he also wants us to run our race *victoriously*!

He, along with that great cloud of witnesses, is cheering us on as we pick ourselves up off the asphalt and get back in the race.

> Don't you realize that in a race everyone runs,
> but only one person gets the prize? So run to win!
> All athletes are disciplined in their training. They
> do it to win a prize that will fade away, but we
> do it for an eternal prize. So I run with purpose
> in every step. I am not just shadowboxing. I
> discipline my body like an athlete, training it to
> do what it should. Otherwise, I fear that after

preaching to others I myself might be disqualified. (1 Cor. 9:24–27)

I love when Paul says, "I'm not just shadowboxing." He isn't
messing around here. In other words, we're not playing games. We
can't waste time. You have a calling and an assignment attached
to your name.

Run with purpose.

Finishing What We Start

If we are going to finish our race well, we too are going to need
every bit of Jesus to cross that finish line. Just as Paul continued
on fighting the good fight and finishing his race despite his wandering, wondering, and wrestling, we too will have to commit to
being ready in season and out of season to make it to the end.

How do we do this?

We cancel the quitting culture.

You might be thinking, that's great, it's catchy, I could buy
into that, but in a world so quick to cancel everything and everyone *how* do we go about canceling the quitting culture?

I wish there was a magic formula, Bible verse, or guarantee
that if we chose to stay and fight, we would always see a victory.
Unfortunately, there is no guarantee. Longevity isn't a free pass to
an easy journey; however, it does allow us to establish roots where
we can say, "We are like trees planted along the riverbank, bearing
fruit each season. Our leaves never wither, and we prosper in all
we do" (see Ps. 1:3).

Roots allow us to develop relationships and personal experiences that teach us how to stay planted when everything in us wants to uproot before God's timing.

Knowing what is coming for those he mentored, and that they too might be tempted to quit, Paul writes to his spiritual son Timothy and instructs him to be prepared to "preach the word of God. Be prepared, whether the time is favorable or not. Patiently correct, rebuke, and encourage your people with good teaching" (2 Tim. 4:2). Some translations say to "be ready in season and out of season."

Much like those volleyball parents cheering from the sidelines for the weary child out on the court, Paul is reminding Timothy he won't always win but he has to finish the game.

Paul continues his pep talk in 2 Timothy 4:5, "Don't be afraid of suffering for the Lord. Work at telling others the Good News, and fully carry out the ministry God has given you." At the end of his life as he faces execution, he looks back and with great confidence declares, "I have finished the race, and I have remained faithful" (v. 7).

Victors, Not Quitters

I believe Paul was fully aware of his own past and sin. He knew he was capable of dropping the ball and losing a game, and if he was going to finish well, he needed every bit of Jesus to make it to the end.

I've often stood in front of the mirror and shook my head at my own shortcomings, sin, and failures and felt Paul's words deeply within my soul.

"I don't really understand myself, for I want to do what is right, but I don't do it. Instead, I do what I hate" (Rom. 7:15).

There are no shortcuts to reaching the end without growing pains, strains, or bruises. Eventually, we all have to take a good look at our reflection and realize we're running with a limp that doesn't disqualify us, rather it gives God access to our weakness, where his power and strength carries us over the finish line as victors, not quitters.

In the winter of 2017, my family was preparing for our move to Colorado Springs for my new position; however, I was still on staff as the worship leader at a wonderful church in Cincinnati. I loved the people and had invested five years growing a team. Though I desired to leave well, I was already mentally packing my house and moving on to a new season.

It seems no matter how well we try to go, we can't always avoid messy endings. I gave my employer a two-month notice to make a smooth transition for the staff and congregants and, soon after, regretted that decision.

One snowy morning I called my mentor, a sweet retired high school principal and spiritual mama who had walked me through several transitions in ministry. I wept as I told her I wanted to be done, that I was tired and overwhelmed and didn't have the energy for drama and drawn-out exits. I hoped she would encourage me to change my plan, turn in a two-week notice and focus on the next few months as we put our house on the market and said thirty-eight years' worth of goodbyes.

Sally didn't give me her blessing. In fact, over the next hour on the phone I felt like a student back in the principal's office as she gently corrected me and challenged me to finish what I had started.

She was teaching me that many of our races are won in the final lap. We can't start a new race if we don't finish the old. How we leave a season, how we exit a position, can impact how we enter the new thing.

If we leave offended, we start defensive.

If we finish weak, we start fragile.

If we quit before our time, we start the new thing with unfinished business.

I didn't want to leave any unfinished business behind in Ohio because I cared too much about those I was leading and those I loved to hurt them with a rushed goodbye or a sloppy leadership handoff.

Much to my personal discomfort and exhaustion, I stayed in my position for another two months and finished my race with that church and my team. It came with personal sacrifice, hard conversations, lengthy explanations, tears, a lot of goodbye dinners, and a few difficult scenarios that grew me as a Christ follower, leader, and friend.

It's not easy leaving those you have cleaved to, those who have raised you and praised you and grazed alongside of you as you fed the flock. Even those who nearly broke you, bruised you, and rebuked you were part of growing you as they just about wore you down. Obedience isn't simple, it's filled with hard goodbyes and unknown tomorrows followed by new hellos and assignments. It costs us familiarity in exchange for anonymity.

Where you are going requires the same mission with a new strategy, soldiers, and stamina. Where you have been prepared you with everything you need to find strength in this new season. Not everyone will understand. Not everyone will be welcoming, but not everyone has been tasked with this responsibility.

So, go with little expectation but great faith and holy anticipation. On the other side of obedience are adventure and people you have been made for and prepared for. I know it's scary, but God has already gone where you are going.

I stayed and finished my assignment even though everything in me wanted to avoid the tension of transition.

You might be asking, how does one leave well even under difficult circumstances? No matter how well we try to go, we can't escape some clumsy exits and shaky narratives as to why and how everything went down behind the scenes.

> Obedience isn't simple, it's filled with hard goodbyes and unknown tomorrows followed by new hellos and assignments.

It's inevitable that people will be sad, maybe even mad or hurt, and that's okay. Not everyone will understand your next God-given assignment.

Sometimes we have to go, and there's nowhere to go.

Sometimes we have to leave, and we have no idea who will drive the getaway car.

No matter the details, we can go well even if we get a little banged up in the process. Honor is a Kingdom currency.

Even when the price feels more expensive than the experience was worth. Pay it, lavish it, pour it out, and then keep
giving where you can.

When God calls you to go, leave the house better than you
found it. How we leave one house is often how we will enter a
new one.

There isn't a perfect exit strategy. But …

- Give your oversight or pastoral covering
  plenty of notice when possible. Two weeks is
  professional, two months is too long.
- Have systems and protocols in place to help
  your successor be successful. Leave them what
  you wish you'd had when you started, such as
  important names, phone numbers, emails, or
  documents in an organized file.
- Promptly return church-issued keys, laptops,
  or other materials to the appropriate depart-
  ments with thank-you cards to those who
  served you behind the scenes.
- Celebrate the good memories in public and
  learn from the bad in private or with a counselor or mentor. If there are concerns of abuse
  or toxic leadership, address those with HR,
  not a peer or congregant.
- Be gracious where grace was shown, be
  thankful for what you were given, forgive

where you can, and let go of what you can't
carry with you.
- Don't carry old dirt into new seasons.

Perhaps you're in the middle of your own transition and it
feels awkward and a little clunky. Or maybe you're being challenged or isolated and your dreams feel as if they've been put on
hold as you wait on your next directive from the Lord.

You've been shaken, pressed, and broken, but you haven't
quit. Not yet anyway. Your lungs are bursting and muscles burning, your heart is exploding as you run an uphill race you didn't
know would be so hard. Yet here you are, head down and eyes
up as you're locking gaze with the one who has numbered your
days and committed to you that he will finish what he asked you
to start.

You are only disqualified from your race if you choose to
quit.

How do you cancel the quitting culture?

You refuse to quit.

You Won't Always Get What You Want

When I was a kid, my mom would never let me leave a friend's
house angry. I was never allowed to pick up my toys and go home
without a come-to-Jesus meeting where there were inevitable tears
and hurt feelings and hugging it out.

In a world filled with,

"no" and,

"almost but not quite," and,
"don't call us we'll call you," and,
"we've decided to go in a different direction ..."
We are faced with two choices:

- we can pick up our toys and try another house,
  or
- we can stick around and find out why it didn't
  work out.

We can learn. Mourn. Grow. This is where we learn to ask the hard questions.

Why this Egypt again?
What do I need to learn from this?
Who do I need to forgive?
From whom do I need to seek forgiveness?

As I watch my generation revolve through the doors of church after church using language like "They didn't give me opportunities to do what gives me life" or "It's just not my passion" or "I couldn't be me," I'm not surprised we lack longevity. Nobody wants to stick around long enough to have the hard conversation, public tears, or hug it out because we've learned we can just avoid accountability and go somewhere else.

If you're only willing to do the things that "give you life," you'll miss out on the opportunities to lay down your life. Hobbies serve us. Following Jesus demands our death before we can truly live.

What if God is letting us go through a growing season and wants us to stay to walk out a no or a new? What if he wants us to learn how to share and play nicely with others even when we feel wronged? What if it feels like a punishment to not get what we want but his "no" made room for a later and greater "YES!"

A new house might have newer toys or what you think comes with better parents, but it also has different rules. Stomping out of one door and into another out of offense or pain or fear will never bring forth good fruit.

This isn't how we fight the good fight or win the race.

Things Church Leaders Say

"I'm just not getting to do what gives me life." Can I make a confession? I've said this more than once or twice in my adult life and it's possible I've written it in my journals in the past five years.

I come to you with good news and not-so-good news. Do you want the good news first? Here it is ...

There will be seasons your passion and your position align and what a sweet spot it is! You will wake up every day and pinch yourself that you get to do what you want to do with the people you get to do it with, and all will seem right in the world.

The not-so-good news?

There are times a shift takes place. A new assignment. A new role. A new ask. Suddenly, what gave you life is demanding your life. Sacrifice. Servanthood. Surrender. Because following Jesus will take you from the wedding feast to the wilderness overnight, but God doesn't change. He's the same when you're at the party as when you're in the pit; we just don't like the scenery as much.

Yet God does miracles in both places.

He's with us when we're living our best life and when we're learning how heavy the cross really is.

It's tempting to quit when we realize the weight of our yes. We say things like "It's not fair, I'm not valued, I don't feel seen, this isn't what I signed up for ..."

"Indeed, I have been crucified with Christ. My ego is no longer central. It is no longer important that I appear righteous before you or have your good opinion, and I am no longer driven to impress God. Christ lives in me. The life you see me living is not 'mine,' but it is lived by faith in the Son of God, who loved me and gave himself for me. I am not going to go back on that" (Gal. 2:20 MSG).

This is exactly what you signed up for and I want to encourage you that laying down your life is much sweeter than you can imagine.

I wish someone would have sat me down in my early twenties to explain my ministry internship job description plus all the other things I wouldn't find hidden in the fine print. Things like, Applicant must:

- be proficient in hard conversations on holy ground.
- expect sweet disappointment and unexpected miracles.
- be prepared for unimaginable heartbreak and willing to contend for reconciliation.
- be ready to receive accountability you don't want and humility that is much needed.

- be prepared to lead difficult people who will become your most loved community.
- be advised that work is both beautiful and brutal. Life-giving and soul-sucking. Both satisfying and full surrender.

By signing on the dotted line, we accept the role of shepherd, janitor, leader, servant, friend, deliverer of hard news, intercessor, mediator, baby holder, first responder, last to leave, meal train maker, the one who marries and often buries.

Welcome to the team.

This is where we find longevity in loving God and his people. This is why we stay, because we learn carrying a cross leads to resurrection, not only in our lives, but in those we get to serve each and every day.

This is the life that gives life.

The Language of Longevity

Staying through challenging circumstances will also teach us a new language and new ways to communicate the heart of Jesus for his Church. When we war beside and survive multiple battles alongside the same people, trust and relational equity are built. We can learn to use different methods of warfare to fight off an enemy.

In my late thirties I entered a new season with a new job description that required me to minister in different ways, fighting new battles where new weapons were required. Maybe you've been there too. You started out in one position that you loved only to be unexpectedly moved to another, and if given the choice, you would have politely declined.

Sometimes God doesn't ask us our opinions; he places us in uncomfortable spaces not to punish us but to move us closer to his plan for our lives.

As a worship leader, I spent twenty years reaching into my arsenal for my weapon of choice, and when I found something in there I didn't know how to use, it terrified and angered me. How would I use it? What was it for? It was so heavy and clunky, it wasn't what I wanted. I remember telling God, "This isn't who I am!"

Everyone knew me as a worship leader and songwriter; I had spent years honing my craft and building relationships and suddenly I was no longer part of the worship community. I felt isolated, unwanted, and replaced.

Growing up in the Pentecostal Church, I understood the musicians and worshippers were on the front lines. I saw worship used as effective warfare against all types of sickness, oppression, and needs. I would read the story of Paul and Silas in their jail cell and feel emboldened to worship with that same tenacity, believing my praise could break chains and set prisoners free.

So when I grew up to become a worship leader and learned to play the piano, I picked up that weapon and never looked back.

This was how I fought my battles.

Worship became one of my greatest tools in fighting off the enemy. I knew how to go into the enemy's camp and take back what he had stolen. I wasn't afraid; I wasn't scared. It was who I was and what I did.

But I learned that my weapon of worship had become my identity.

My weapon had become an idol.

The Lord, in his goodness to us, will ask us to hand over anything and everything that we exalt over him and his will. He gives us the choice to surrender it or have him pry it from our cold, dead hands. I've learned surrender is the better option. If I'm honest, it's been a long season of learning how to use new weaponry, but let me tell you something I wish I had known:

He is training our hands for warfare, so the more weapons, the more tools in our tool belt, the sharper we become in using the old and learning the new. He is waking us up with new strategy, giving us new vision, and making us more creative in how we use our gifts by his grace, not our personal talent.

He is using us to confuse an enemy who has never seen us fight this way before.

I get it. You love that weapon; I love my keyboard. I know you handpicked that tool, but I have good news. God handpicked you! He is going to ask you to fight a new battle with a new weapon, and you need to know it will be one of the greatest moments of your life when you learn how to use it for his glory.

Not because it's your first choice or because it's the popular weapon everyone is picking up, but because he is trusting you with more.

I want to encourage you to search your heart and seek the voice of your Father in the days ahead. Spend time in prayer, fast, journal, go to counseling, and dare to confront the idols that are keeping you from stepping into new territories.

What no or rejection are you wrestling with right now? What yes are you avoiding? What opportunities have you turned down because you didn't like your options or felt unfamiliar with the tools being handed to you? What if God is inviting you into a new territory or a new season where his goodness and favor will surround you, but you haven't let go of what you've always done and who you've always been?

What Egypt does God continue to put back in your path that you can't seem to escape? Pay attention. Sometimes God sends us back to uncomfortable places to demonstrate his great power and purpose in our lives.

What Felt Like Exile Was Actually an Exodus

Admittedly, a toxic trait of mine is my knee-jerk reaction to quit before I get hurt. Most of my life, I have had this mentality that if I reject a person or position before that person or position cancels me, then I remain in control. As I mentioned earlier, self-preservation is not a fruit of the Spirit. Self-preservation causes us to panic, to make irrational decisions and to protect ourselves from things that aren't even threats. It's a false sense of security.

Many of us fear rejection from our peers more than disobedience to God. We are so afraid of being isolated, forgotten, or irrelevant that we quit rather than stay long enough to find out why God is asking us to walk out a hard relationship, lesson, or assignment. Like my daughter's volleyball team, we start with holy determination to win but after a few mistakes become discouraged and defeated.

What if our failures and shortcomings didn't disqualify us from the race, rather they were used to train us to run with more wisdom and strategy? What if we actually learned from every fall and obstacle?

What if what the enemy wanted us to think was exile was actually an exodus?

Is it possible …

You weren't rejected. You were rescued.

The word *exodus* from the Greek word *Exodos* means "the road out," and some of us need to hear that what has felt like rejection was actually a holy rescue. What has felt like a season of exile was a stealthy mission of a good Father who loves you too much to let your need for acceptance lead to your captivity.

> Self-preservation causes us to panic, to make irrational decisions and to protect ourselves from things that aren't even threats.

God knows when it's time for a departure or our outgoing long before we sense a change. And we might have to wander in a wilderness for a bit, but we always find a parting sea and the promises of God fulfilled, because his promises are yes and amen.

It's here, in uncomfortable places, we learn to take the land entrusted to us. It won't take you forty years because once you hear the voice of God you won't second-guess him like you did the first time. Yes, rejection and offense often feel like exile, but with each transition and new season you'll know when it's time to take all the favor given to you and get out of Egypt.

Nobody wants to go back to their Egypt. Yet in revisiting these areas that keep holding us prisoner, we learn to break free from the things keeping us from the Promised Land.

We all want things to be easy, to go our way. As Christians, we don't like to wrestle or be seen wandering in a wilderness we should have already tamed. But quitting every time something gets hard will keep us from stepping into the promises of God.

The mission before us requires a staff in one hand and the commandments of God in the other, and not everyone will understand what it is God has asked us to carry. So yes, there will be seasons of isolation and loneliness.

But isolation and loneliness aren't an excuse to quit, rather an invitation from our Father to press in and rest in his presence.

You are never alone.

Carry what God has given you up that mountain, run that race, and do it all in his glory.

What has felt like a season of exile can be your exodus as you walk in obedience. Others are watching you and waiting for you to finish what you started, and it might even help them find their way to a miracle.

Grab your backpack. It's time to take some land.

CHAPTER 12

I'M STILL HERE

"Do you know why birds sing just before dawn?
Scientists believe it's to tell their mates that they made
it through the night, as a way of saying, 'I'm still here.'
Maybe that's why we sing, too, why we create art—as
a way of saying, 'I made it. I'm still here.'"[22]

Jeff Goins

The familiar humidity of Ohio in August smacked me in the face as I stepped out of the rental car, my high heels clacking on the pavement below. I gently closed the driver door and walked to the other side to get a better look at the property, much smaller than I remembered. The lot where our church parsonage had sat was now just an empty green square, a little rectangular driveway the only evidence a home once occupied the space.

Nostalgia is a haunting human phenomenon producing a powerful wave of emotions with the potential to either crush us or propel us forward. Amy Bloom wrote, "The past is a candle at great distance: too close to let you quit, too far to comfort you."[23]

As I stood there in the hot sun, one month shy of my forty-second birthday, nearly twenty-five years since the day our family pulled out of this very parking lot and said goodbye to our home and church family, I could hear echoes of laughter wrapped up in the wind.

Like an old movie unfolding before my eyes, our old brick ranch gradually appeared in front of the setting sun. I saw the back porchlight burning bright where I had my first kiss good-night in high school. I watched as toilet paper magically wrapped up the trees where my friends had pulled an epic prank one night while we slept. I heard the booming voices of the elder board, most of whom have gone on to meet Jesus, shooting off funny jabs at one another as they loaded into their cars after a late-night board meeting. The old blue church bus that hauled me to camps and church conferences in my most formative years where my friends and I sang old Point of Grace songs in four-part harmony, and threw candy from windows during the town Fourth of July parade, sat like an abandoned amusement-park ride in its usual parking spot near the storage shed.

I turned to my right to see the church, the signature architectural point of the sanctuary piercing into the sky like the mast of the *Titanic*, and the stained-glass windows twinkling in the evening sun. The main doors where I used to let myself in to play piano after school, or to lie on my dad's cool office floor while he studied on hot summer days, were wide open as if to say, "Welcome home, old friend," and I could smell my adolescence wafting out in the air-conditioned mist.

I walked toward the open doors, and in that moment, I realized what had felt like being sent into exile by people we had loved was actually an exodus provided by God. He had protected my family and me, sent us out on a new assignment and rerouted our course to avoid deadly shipwrecks that might have marooned us for life. I wasn't the same teenage girl who left confused and bitter. I was healed and whole. I took a step onto that familiar carpet, squared my shoulders, and put the enemy on notice.

I'm still here.

The Song We Will Sing

As we close out our time together, I pray you can hear my song in the night. I'm still here. You're still here. We made it. Albeit a little bruised and banged up, but we're still singing even if it is taking all our strength to whisper out a song. Forgive me, forgive the Church, forgive others if we have made ministry or walking with Jesus look easy. The truth is, following Jesus is beautiful, and the journey at times brutal, and he is found in both the beauty and the brokenness.

Throughout all of Scripture, we see Jesus meeting people where they are on their journeys. From a well to a sycamore tree, to pits and palaces, shipwrecks and face to face with our enemy in a cave, his eyes are always upon us. He says things like "Come to me, all of you who are weary ... and I will give you rest" (Matt. 11:28) and "Give all your worries and cares to God, for he cares about you" (1 Pet. 5:7) and again in Matthew 11 verse 30, "For my yoke is easy to bear, and the burden I give you is light."

He knew there would be days we would lose our song.

When we say yes to Jesus and loving his people, we'll have some sleepless nights, days of beating our fists into the air and crying out in hopelessness, but we don't see that on social media. Pastors and leaders are quick to post smiling selfies surrounded by groups filled with laughter, when in reality our insides are falling apart. So many leaders appear to be suited up with ball in hand when in reality they are ready to quit the game.

Maybe if we were all really honest, we'd realize that we're all in a similar war. We're not alone, we're not crazy. Perhaps in hearing the stories of others wanting to quit and choosing to stay, we'd admit the struggle to walk away from our faith and calling is real, but we have a God who saves us and who is fighting for us on our most war-weary days. We would most likely find we do have an army in each other, and we don't have to quit.

If I'm honest with you, and I think I can be after our time here together, I have no idea if I'm doing this following Jesus and loving people well. I just know that I can't quit, and trust me, I want to quit nearly every single day. So I'll commit to you that I'll finish this race, but I'm going to be honest with you when I don't want to. Please do the same. This isn't supposed to be easy; it's going to be messy, but it's what leads us back to Jesus every single time.

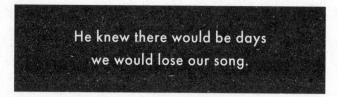

He knew there would be days
we would lose our song.

You're going to want it to be easy, but nothing good comes without some resistance. You'll want the race without the exhaustion, the fight without a worthy opponent, the ministry without the wrestle, but know this ...

The battle is where things start to happen, where our lives are changed, where our strategies are challenged, and our identity is mocked as we learn the battles of today cannot be fought or won with yesterday's anointing, yesterday's song.

We win a today war with a today word.

So if you want to partner with God in defeating the enemy, if you want to see the Kingdom of God win, you have to engage in the war. This is where we learn to pray without ceasing and to worship in the warfare and to fast even when our bodies feel as if they will fail us.

Every victory starts with a battle.

Each win starts with a war.

Against good and evil, our own flesh and blood and the will of God, our voice and his voice, the word of the world and the Word of God.

We can't fight this war behind a computer screen or in our shower where we daydream of destroying our accusers with harsh rhetoric. Because we aren't fighting people or even each other, it's much bigger, so our weapons must be much bigger than tweets among twits.

In our attempt to avoid pain and further heartbreak, we often run so far from his voice that all we can hear is our own heavy breathing and the lie of our enemy, who has one goal: to kill us and take our voice. He wants to steal our song and our testimony that declare to everyone around us we aren't finished yet. Satan hates the melodic worship that exudes from the brokenness of our lives because it reminds him that he lost and will never defeat our living God.

As we have learned from our brothers Paul and Joseph and many others who have gone before us, the song we have been given to sing over our lives as the redeemed is one of redemption, reconciliation, and forgiveness that we only learn through persecution, patience, and perseverance.

If we quit, we won't ever hear the whole song.

The Song of Legacy

As I stepped through the familiar doors of the church and made the turn into the sanctuary that had raised me all those years ago, I was overcome with emotion. On the stage stood friends old and new, those who had been there when we said goodbye and those who had only heard of it. We were all coming together for a special weekend: the church's one-hundred-year anniversary.

I was invited to lead worship by a former youth group friend, the current pastor's wife, who I found scurrying around with her own children in tow setting up and giving directions. I could still remember her as an eleven-year-old, dressed as an angel in the Christmas cantata, her little curls dropping into her eyes from under the halo. I couldn't help but envy her; she had found legacy in this house and in this family we once shared.

After several hugs and introductions on the platform, and what seemed like hours going down memory lane, we began our rehearsal of old gospel favorites from over the years as people trickled in.

As if the seats were supernaturally assigned, I watched as the saints filed in. I would have sworn when I was fifteen that they must have been eighty, but here they came now truly in their eighties to take their positions in their favorite pews wearing their familiar perfumes. Some saw me from afar and, as if they were seeing a ghost, shuffled their way to me, cradled my face in their wrinkled hands, and stared deep into my soul with watery eyes.

"Natalie? Is that you? You look just like your daddy ..."

"Honey? Could it be? What a beauty you are ..."

It was almost too much to bear. These spiritual moms and dads found me one at a time, the gruff voices catching me off guard as they asked if my parents were coming and told me old stories of a time I had tried to forget.

"Your dad was my favorite hunting buddy ..."

"Tell your mom we miss her singing ..."

By the time I got up to the platform I had come undone, and as I looked out over the sanctuary, I didn't see my critics, I recognized a family I had dearly missed.

The pastor came to the platform to welcome the crowd—many who had attended for fifty-plus years and others who were visiting after some time away. He took a moment to introduce those of us leading worship, listing the years served followed by polite clapping and a few cheers as each name was called. When he got to me, he didn't introduce me as a worship leader, he introduced me as Pastor Ron's daughter, a pastor whom they had all loved and who had been a personal mentor and friend to him.

At the mention of my dad's name, you heard an audible gasp as those who had known us leaned in for a closer look and began putting my face with my dad's name. Then, something unforgettable happened. The room erupted into applause.

They had loved us. They still loved us.

They didn't hate us. They weren't disappointed in me.

They were still our family. We weren't forgotten.

The pastor looked back at me, red cheeked and pushing back tears.

He said, "When I first started in ministry, your dad, Pastor Ron, hired me as his youth pastor. He would put me in the car, and we would drive through the city, and he would weep and pray over the neighborhoods. Natalie, tell your dad I caught his heart."

I was speechless. My dad had left a legacy. He wasn't remembered as the guy who left, he was remembered as the guy who loved. Marcel Proust once said, "Remembrance of things past is not necessarily the remembrance of this as they were."[24]

It is true. What I remembered through a lens of hurt and bitterness was not actually true. Through the lens of a healed heart, I could find the beauty over the brokenness.

I wished more than anything my dad had come with me; I wanted him to hear for himself how much he had meant to this church and the people. I wanted him to hear this song of legacy. That his sacrifice had meant something, and his name was held dear by those who loved him.

If I would've quit, if I would've let my wandering and wondering and wrestling lead me away from Jesus and ministry, I would have never found myself twenty-five years later on a platform to hear these words and witness this celebration.

If we quit, we won't hear the song of redemption. We won't know the melody of restoration. We won't sing the song of reconciliation. The enemy wants us to quit because he wants the family of God to divorce; he wants nothing more than to separate us.

The Ministry of Quitting

Our enemy has one ministry: to destroy God's children. He wants us to quit because he knows what happens when Kingdom assignments are fulfilled: crosses are carried, and graves are emptied.

Since the garden the enemy has been trying to make us question what we know God has spoken over us. From his infamous question to Eve, "Did God really say that?" to tempting Jesus in the desert, his goal has always been to place doubt toward our Father in our hearts.

He didn't want Adam and Eve fulfilling their God-given mandate in the garden to fill the earth with people and command with purpose. He wanted Jesus taken down too, but what he didn't count on was a plot twist where the cross would become his own demise.

His goal and tactics, though basic and unoriginal, still seem to catch us by surprise. It's as if we think the work we're doing couldn't possibly be enough to make us a target. After all, we're not populating the earth or saving mankind.

We have to remember: his entire goal is to get us to question God and quit our assignment. When he lost the keys to the Kingdom, we became his greatest threat as he saw for himself what happens when God finishes what he starts through his people.

Crosses get carried.

Veils are torn.

Graves are emptied.

So, of course, he doesn't want us picking up our cross and following Jesus because with every cross we carry there are those to our right or left coming with us, and the result is always resurrection.

Reconciliation.

Restoration.

Eternal life.

Every. Single. Time.

His warfare may be predictable and cheap, but he's taking down a lot of us simply by making us question the voice of our Creator. He's taking us down in desert places with a glass of water filled with salt, and I'm here to sound the alarm: don't drink from that cup.

I don't know what you're about to question or quit, but here are a few reminders for us all:

What God says he means.

"This truth gives them confidence that they have eternal life, which God—who does not lie— promised them before the world began" (Titus 1:2).

What God promises is true.

"For all of God's promises have been fulfilled in Christ with a resounding 'Yes!' And through

Christ, our 'Amen' (which means 'Yes') ascends to God for his glory" (2 Cor. 1:20).

What God starts he finishes.

"And I am certain that God, who began the good work within you, will continue his work until it is finally finished on the day when Christ Jesus returns" (Phil. 1:6).

What God calls us to he will equip us for in due season.

"So let's not get tired of doing what is good. At just the right time we will reap a harvest of blessing if we don't give up" (Gal. 6:9).

Remember: our enemy knows a carried cross means an emptied grave.

Don't abandon the cross.

If you take anything away from this entire book, hear these words flowing from my own life ... when we stay, we find the Jesus we have always wanted to know and a family worth fighting for with every fiber of our being.

We stay for Jesus. We stay to remember that original yes to a God who loves us and a family that isn't perfect but it's ours.

We will shipwreck ourselves over and over and find ourselves in pits and prisons and taken for granted in palaces, but God is still working out all things for our good, so we have to stay and see his plan through.

Finishing What He Started

When our family made the move from Ohio to Colorado Springs in early 2017, we drove through the evangelical suburb getting to know our new home and pulled up to a giant building with a familiar name. It was the headquarters of the very popular ministry and publisher where I had sent my first book back in college, the one who gently rejected me with a handwritten note, "Your story isn't finished yet."

I stared through the window like a little girl seeing Disneyland for the first time, wide eyed and a little emotional. I hadn't thought about the book in a really long time, and suddenly, I had this urge to dig through all our unpacked boxes to find that ancient manuscript. Our girls jumped out of the car to run around the large campus, and I stayed behind as the last twenty-five years came to a screeching halt behind me. In the cool Colorado air, I am quite sure I heard the audible voice of a Jesus who didn't let me quit say, "We will finish what we started here."

If you would have told me at eighteen years old that it would take another twenty-five years for my heart to heal and mature before this book would be written, I probably would have quit right there in my dorm room. I would've saved myself the fifty dollars on my dining card and a scary midnight bike ride to a printing lab and a whole lot of rejection. As wounded as I was, as hurt as I had been by the church, something in me still believed God wasn't finished with me just yet.

He's not finished with you just yet either.

> We stay for Jesus. We stay to remember
> that original yes to a God who loves us
> and a family that isn't perfect but it's ours.

Each of us could go back to a time in our lives when we wanted to quit, probably multiple times, and yet the song we sing is "I'm still here." I can hear your song. I'm singing it with you right now. This book ... the ministry of Raised to Stay ... is simply a reminder to us all, "And I am certain that God, who began the good work within you, will continue his work until it is finally finished on the day when Christ Jesus returns" (Phil. 1:6).

We are the sea weary, pit survivors, palace dwellers, wilderness walkers who aren't looking for platforms. Rather we are willing to take a pilgrimage and we know the difference between the two. I see our generation, the fire walkers, unbothered by the heat beneath our feet. We will reject temporary spotlights and choose a holy longevity over five minutes of fame.

I hear new voices and songs and messages forged from days under the sun in search of living water. Our patient endurance, our resolution to finish our race, to walk out of our wilderness, to stay will introduce another generation to a Jesus we know and a Church we love. Our voices will carry an eternal echo not because we're famous but because we are the pioneers who unashamedly declare, "Prepare the way for the LORD's coming! Clear the road for him!" (Mark 1:3).

Quitting will not be our legacy. We will be generations known for our passionate pursuit of Christ and fulfilling the Great Commission. We will be remembered for loving one another, forgiving one another, persevering, and our hunger for the presence of God. We will tell stories and share testimonies of what should have crushed us, but instead of being consumed by a wildfire of bitterness and resentment, we used those experiences as kindling for new songs, messages, books, and lessons. We aren't quitters. We are the stayers.

This is our song and the song we will sing over generations to come.

We are raised to stay.

NOTES

1. J. R. R. Tolkien, "The Riddle of Strider" in *The Fellowship of the Ring*, The Lord of the Rings (New York: Random House, 1986), 193.

2. "Jon Foreman: The Switchfoot Man Talks about 'Fall,' 'Winter,' 'Spring,' and 'Summer,'" interview with Mike Rimmer and Tony Cummings, July 2, 2008, www.crossrhythms.co.uk/articles/music /Jon_Foreman_The_Switchfoot_man_talks_about_Fall_Winter _Spring_and_Summer_/32165/p1/.

3. *Merriam-Webster Online Dictionary*, s.v. "remnant," accessed November 4, 2022, www.merriam-webster.com/dictionary /remnant.

4. Lester V. Meyer, "Remnant," *Anchor Yale Bible Dictionary*, vol. 5, 8th ed. (New Haven, CT: Yale University Press, 1992), 669.

5. Brennan Manning, *The Ragamuffin Gospel: Good News for the Bedraggled, Beat-Up, and Burnt Out* (Portland, OR: Multnomah, 1990), 25.

6. Roy Hattersley, *Blood and Fire: William and Catherine Booth and Their Salvation Army* (New York: Doubleday, 2000), 25.

7. C. H. Spurgeon, "Sin and Grace," sermon, Metropolitan Tabernacle, London, November 1, 1874, Spurgeon Archive, accessed November 5, 2022, https://archive.spurgeon.org/sermons/3115.php.

8. Krysten Swensen, "Guardians of the Galaxy—Mission: BREAKOUT! at Disneyland Resort," Inside the Magic, June 26, 2021, https://insidethemagic.net/2021/06/guide-to-guardians-of-the-galaxy-mission-breakout-ks1mmb/.

9. Linda Dillow, *Satisfy My Thirsty Soul: For I Am Desperate for Your Presence* (Colorado Springs: NavPress, 2014), 40.

10. John Bevere, *The Bait of Satan: Living Free from the Deadly Trap of Offense*, 20th anniv. ed. (Lake Mary, FL: Charisma House, 2014), 6.

11. Kris Vallotton, "Humility Is Still the Way Forward," KrisVallotton.com, November 13, 2020, www.krisvallotton.com/humility-is-still-the-way-forward.

12. Bevere, *Bait of Satan*, 14.

13. Robert H. Schuller, quoted at Pass It On, accessed November 6, 2022, www.passiton.com/inspirational-quotes/7580-let-your -hopes-not-your-hurts-shape-your-future.

14. Steve Cuss, *Managing Leadership Anxiety: Yours and Theirs* (Nashville, TN: Thomas Nelson, 2019), 63.

15. Kris Vallotton and Bill Johnson, *The Supernatural Ways of Royalty: Discovering Your Rights and Privileges of Being a Son or Daughter of God* (Shippensburg, PA: Destiny Image, 2017), 86.

16. Lisa Bevere, *Godmothers: Why You Need One. How to Be One* (Grand Rapids, MI: Revell, 2020), 154.

17. Dorothy Draper, quoted in *Smithsonian Makers Workshop: Fascinating History and Essential How-Tos: Gardening, Crafting, Decorating, and Food* (New York: HarperCollins, 2020), 193.

18. *Kid 90*, directed by Soleil Moon Frye (Burbank, CA: STX Entertainment, 2021).

19. Gretchen Anthony, *The Kids Are Going to Ask* (New York: Park Row, 2020).

20. Alexander Maclaren, "Ecclesiastes 7:8," in *Maclaren's Expositions of Holy Scripture* (Grand Rapids, MI: Eerdmans, 1959).

21. Claire Colvin, "I Am a Citizen of This World, So This IS My Fight," *SheLovesMagazine.com*, February 21, 2017, https://shelovesmagazine.com/2017/this-is-my-fight/.

22. Jeff Goins, @JeffGoins, "Do you know why birds …," Twitter, May 13, 2019, 7:21 a.m., https://twitter.com/jeffgoins/status /1127896570379362304?lang=en.

23. Amy Bloom, *Away* (New York: Random House, 2007), 186.

24. Marcel Proust, *In Search of Lost Time (Remembrance of Things Past)*, 6 vols. (France: Grasset and Gallimard, 1922–1931).

BIBLE CREDITS